Life's Sweetest Moments

Life's Sweetest Moments

SIMPLE, STUNNING RECIPES AND THEIR HEARTWARMING STORIES

DOMINIQUE ANSEL

PHOTOGRAPHS BY EVAN SUNG

HARVEST

An Imprint of WILLIAM MORROW

HarperCollins books may be purchased for educational, business, or sales promotional use. For information, please email the Special Markets Department at SPsales@harpercollins.com.

FIRST EDITION

Designed by Renata DiBiase
Photographs by Evan Sung

Library of Congress Cataloging-in-Publication Data has been applied for.

ISBN 978-0-06-330809-1

24 25 26 27 28 IMG 10 9 8 7 6 5 4 3 2 1

My little family. One smile and I melt.

Contents

Introduction

A PASTRY IS never *just* a pastry.

Pastries have been a ticket for me into the lives and memories of so many people who have walked through our bakery doors. You see a cake or a tart in our pastry case, but I see something entirely different: a gift, a first date, a reunion. Behind every dessert, there is a story to share.

Over the years, I have seen marriage proposals over a cup of rich hot chocolate with marshmallows that melt into a silky foam on top. There have been moments of love. But also ones of loss and comfort, change, and farewell. I've watched kids (including my own) grow up, I've said my goodbyes, and I've had countless little encounters that forever changed me. Some of the people you'll read stories about are ones I can't recall by name; others have become lifelong friends.

This cookbook isn't organized the same way most others are. Instead of having categories of desserts, it's divided up into themes and time periods in our lives for which I share some of the stories closest to my heart and the corresponding recipes that were inspired by them. We don't bake just with our hands, but with our heart and soul. And until you bake that in and share those stories, the recipes are incomplete. There's a beautiful tart studded with strawberries inspired by a husband-and-wife duo who would gift each other sweet treats every morning and every night. A moist and tart lemon cake inspired by rainy days, peaches soaking up Sauternes and floating in an ice bath from my childhood, and sugar-dusted beignets that I make every winter. And even a silky crème brûlée inspired by the most unexpected of subjects. My hope is when you make and eat these recipes, you are also living the legacies that they come from.

I've always said that dessert, unlike an entrée or main course, is optional. The reason behind *why* someone orders a dessert is the glimmer that I look for every day. It can be a grand occasion or just a passing impulse. Life, incredibly and thankfully, is filled with countless sweet moments.

CHAPTER 1
The Early Days

Moving to a new city, finding new passions, and starting a new job—these "firsts" are often the moments for a beginner cook to find a reason to bake!

BREAKING OUT OF YOUR SHELL
CRÈME BRÛLÉE

IF SOMEONE TOLD me I would someday need a bouncer for my bakery, I would have laughed. But in 2013, that's exactly who was standing outside the bakery door.

"Everybody, listen up!" The bouncer's voice sounded loudly on the quiet block of Spring Street. The growing line of more than one hundred people provided a captive audience that quickly became a magnet for unwanted solicitors and potential arguments, as well as a sore spot for neighborhood residents who wanted to keep the sidewalk clear. Inside, our small team of just four people hustled to prepare the famous item they were all waiting for: the Cronut®—a half-croissant, half-doughnut pastry that shook up the culinary world . . . and mine.

"Move back against the wall," the bouncer continued.

Around the third day of him shouting, I couldn't shake the feeling that while he kept things in order, this wasn't the level of hospitality I condoned. I sat him down after his morning shift for a late breakfast, and placed the Cronut pastry in front of him. I spoke to him about how our team examines each one every morning for quality control. It takes three days to make a Cronut, from mixing the dough to laminating to cutting, proofing, and frying. Plus, we change the flavor every month and the flavors never repeat.

"Food," I said, "is a great connector of people. We need to make sure we celebrate that, and welcome folks rather than push them away."

The next morning, like clockwork, our bouncer stepped outside to greet our guests. "Yo, everybody, listen up!" he shouted. I sighed. It seemed as if our talk didn't change his tone of voice. But just as I was headed back into the kitchen, I stopped in my tracks. "So, the flava of the Cronut for this month is Blackberry Lime," he continued in his thick Bronx accent. "And I think the lime ganache is silky and refreshing when paired with the blackberry jam." He looked over at me from the corner of his eye and gave me a quick nod. It was, in those hectic and overwhelming times, a moment of triumph I will always remember.

That day marked the making of a new foodie. Over the next few weeks, our bouncer and I would regularly talk about new restaurants that were opening, our favorite home recipes, and whether or not our moms were good cooks (mine was not; his was).

On one of his last days of work with us, he asked me what he should make for dessert for his wife. After some thought, I answered: crème brûlée, a soft baked custard speckled with vanilla topped with a thin burnt-sugar crust. It is a timeless French classic that is easy to execute but always brings a sense of finesse to the table. The list of ingredients is simple, but the trick is all about watching the temperature of each ingredient as you combine them. When you apply a careful touch, everything blends together into a smooth and delicate custard. It's the perfect introductory recipe for any new food appreciator wanting to step up their baking game. And also, I added, he should make it because it reminded me of him: there's a hard shell on the outside that eventually breaks to reveal a soft interior.

MAKES 6 TO 8 SERVINGS

INGREDIENTS

40 grams	1 large	egg
154 grams	8 large	egg yolks
80 grams	6½ tablespoons	sugar
350 grams	1½ cups	whole milk
350 grams	1½ cups	heavy cream

Vanilla seeds (scraped from 1 vanilla bean) or ½ teaspoon vanilla extract

Granulated sugar, for brûléeing the tops

EQUIPMENT

Large bowl	Baking dish: large enough to fit the ramekins (see below) spaced 3 inches (7.5 cm) apart
Whisk	6 shallow crème brûlée ramekins: 5 inches (13 cm) in diameter and 1 inch (2.5 cm) deep
Kettle or medium pot	Kitchen torch

1. Make the custard: In a large bowl, whisk together the whole egg, egg yolks, and sugar. Whisk in the milk, heavy cream, and vanilla seeds (or extract).

2. Prepare a water bath: In a kettle or pot, boil enough water to fill about half the depth of a baking dish that can comfortably fit all the ramekins.

3. Preheat the oven to 285°F (140°C).

4. Bake the custards: Place 6 shallow crème brûlée ramekins (5 inches/13 cm in diameter) into a deep rectangular baking dish, spaced about 3 inches (7.5 cm) apart. Pour the boiling water into the baking dish until it comes three-quarters of the way up the sides of the ramekins (be careful not to get water into the ramekins themselves). Now pour the custard batter into each ramekin until they're full to the top. Bake until the custard is just set, 25 to 30 minutes.

5. Chill: Carefully lift the baked custard ramekins from the water bath and let cool. Once cooled, refrigerate them until they're chilled, about 1 hour. The custard should be jiggly but set in the middle.

6. Brûlée the custards: Just before serving, remove the custards from the fridge. For each ramekin, using a teaspoon or your fingers, sprinkle a small pile of granulated sugar in the center. Turning the ramekin, tap out the excess sugar so that just a thin layer remains. Torch the sugar with a small kitchen torch, gently moving it in small circles so as not to burn the sugar. Repeat the process again with another layer of sugar to caramelize a second time. Wait 2 to 3 minutes for the sugar to cool and then serve.

STORAGE

Best enjoyed immediately.

MILK CHOCOLATE HUMBLE PIE

IT'S AMAZING HOW much insight you can get from thirty-five characters. That's how long the message on our cake plaques can be. In the back of our kitchen, our chef rolls a small cornet out of parchment paper, spoons in a dollop of melted chocolate, and delicately pipes out the message in cursive. Suddenly, the cake has a voice.

"Happy 100th Birthday, Great-Grandpa" brought an extra-wide smile to my face. What a night that must have been with generations coming together to celebrate a milestone. Each letter added more color to the picture, and more heart to the flavors.

Curiously, once in a while a different type of message would surface. The first one that I noticed simply said: "I'm sorry I forgot." A few months later, we spotted a "Please forgive me." And even one that said: "I hope we can still be friends." It never occurred to me that cakes could be messengers for apologies.

To be honest, I was a little skeptical. Would I really forgive someone because they got me a pastry?

One day, I decided I would ask. A guest had come to pick up her cake decorated with a "I'm sorry for being grumpy" plaque. "Are you receiving the apology or giving it?" I asked. She explained she was the apologizer, not the apologizee, and she was bringing it to a coworker.

When asked whether she thought this was effective, she smiled. "Well, I love pastries and they always make me feel better. So, I know people who know me will understand the sincerity behind this." She looked lovingly at the chocolate silk pie that she had chosen, her version of a "humble pie." Layers of chocolate on top of chocolate decadence, the star being the rich ganache filling, which carries with it the hopes of smoothing out any argument. It's a recipe that takes a little planning ahead to make each component—from the chocolate sablé pie dough to the ganache filling to finally the vanilla whipped cream on top. It is built from the bottom up, with the darkest chocolate flavor in the crust and the lightest peaks of cream on the top.

"Worse comes to worst, I'll eat it. I've got a sweet tooth," she said before heading out. "And for that, I'm never sorry."

MAKES 1 PIE (SERVES 6 TO 8)

INGREDIENTS

Chocolate Sablé Crust

80 grams	⅔ cup	powdered sugar
24 grams	¼ cup	unsweetened cocoa powder
200 grams	1½ cups	all-purpose flour
7 grams	1¼ teaspoons	salt
140 grams	1 stick + 2 tablespoons (5 oz)	unsalted butter, at room temperature
50 grams	1 large	egg

Softened unsalted butter, for the pie pan

Milk Chocolate Ganache

130 grams	½ cup + 1 tablespoon	whole milk
229 grams	1 cup	heavy cream
104 grams	5 large	egg yolks
76 grams	⅓ cup	granulated sugar
330 grams	2½ cups	chopped milk chocolate
104 grams	½ cup	water
17 grams	2½ tablespoons	unsweetened cocoa powder

Vanilla Whipped Cream

500 grams	2 cups + 2 tablespoons	heavy cream, well chilled*
50 grams	¼ cup	granulated sugar

Vanilla seeds (scraped from 1 vanilla bean) or ½ teaspoon vanilla extract

Assembly

Cocoa powder or chocolate shavings, for garnish

Make sure your cream is cold. If it's room temperature or warm, it won't whip up into fluffy peaks.

EQUIPMENT

Stand mixer (or hand mixer)

Small bowl

Rolling pin

10-inch (25 cm) pie pan (can be metal, glass, or ceramic)

Paring knife

Parchment paper

Pie weights (or uncooked rice or dried beans)

Medium pot

Large heatproof bowl

Digital thermometer

Immersion blender

Rubber spatula

MAKE THE CHOCOLATE SABLÉ CRUST

1. Mix the dough: In a stand mixer fitted with the paddle (or in a large bowl with a hand mixer), combine the powdered sugar, cocoa powder, flour, salt, and butter. Mix on low speed until the ingredients are well combined and the texture resembles sand, just a few minutes.

2. In a small bowl, beat the egg. Add to the bowl and mix until fully incorporated and the dough is smooth. Do not overmix.

3. Chill the dough: Turn the dough out onto a large piece of plastic wrap and shape it into a ball. Wrap in the plastic and flatten into a disc (flattening the dough helps it chill faster). Refrigerate for at least 1 to 2 hours (or up to overnight), until cold but still pliable. It should have the texture of clay. The dough can be made the day before, then rolled and baked the next day.

4. Position a rack in the center of the oven and preheat the oven to 320°F (160°C).

5. Roll out the dough: Make sure the dough is cold before rolling it out. Using dough that's too warm will cause it to stick to your work surface and the crust will shrink as it bakes. Flour your work surface and rolling pin.* Unwrap the chilled dough and roll out to a large round about ⅛ inch (3 mm) thick and 11½ inches (29 cm) in diameter. Be sure to work quickly so the dough doesn't get too warm. If you notice the dough is sticking to the rolling pin or work surface, add some more flour. You can also rewrap it in plastic and return it to the fridge for 15 to 20 minutes, or even put it in the freezer for 5 minutes, until chilled again.

recipe continues

* You can also roll out the dough between two pieces of parchment paper, which will make it easier to lift up and lay into your pie pan later.

6. Cut the dough: Using your 10-inch (25 cm) pie pan as a guide, cut the dough into a round that's 1½ to 2 inches (4 to 5 cm) wider than the top of the pan (the width of the dough round will depend on the depth of your pan). This ensures the dough will reach up the sides.

7. Fonçage the dough: Now the fun part—fonçaging, or forming the dough into a pie shape. Butter the pie pan. Place the round of chilled dough on top and push down gently with your fingers, pressing along the inside of the pan and into the inside edge (don't press too hard, as you want the dough to have an even thickness so it bakes evenly). Use a paring knife to trim away any excess dough hanging over the sides of the pan, leaving about a ⅓-inch (1 cm) overhang. Fold the dough under itself onto the flat rim of the pie pan.

8. Flute the edges: To "flute"—or crimp—the edges of your pie shell, push the dough with your thumb from one hand in between the thumb and index finger of the opposite hand. Continue to work your way around until you've crimped the entire crust.

9. Blind-bake* the pie shell: Line the pie shell with a round of parchment paper (a large coffee filter works, too!). The surface of the dough—including the sides—should be completely covered. Fill the crust with pie weights (or uncooked rice or dried beans) to keep the dough in place.

* Since the filling for this pie doesn't require baking, you'll need to bake the pie crust in advance of filling it. This is called blind-baking.

10. Bake for 25 minutes. Remove the parchment/coffee filter and the weights/rice/beans, return to the pie crust to the oven, and continue baking until there are no more wet spots on the surface of the dough, another 8 to 10 minutes. The dark color of the dough makes it hard to tell when the crust is done baking. To avoid overbaking, check the crust periodically; if there are no wet spots, it's ready.

11. Cool the pie crust: Remove the pie crust from the oven and let cool fully in the pie pan.* As your pie crust is cooling, make the milk chocolate ganache.

  Before you start assembling your pie, always make sure the crust is fully cooled. If the crust is too hot, the cream will melt and soak into the crust, giving you a soggy-bottomed pie.

MAKE THE MILK CHOCOLATE GANACHE

12. Heat the milk and cream: In a medium pot, bring the milk and cream to a simmer over medium heat, stirring occasionally with a whisk. Do not boil. Once the mixture reaches a simmer, remove from the heat.

13. Temper the eggs: In a bowl, whisk together the egg yolks and granulated sugar until evenly combined. While whisking, slowly pour about one-third of the heated milk mixture into the egg mixture to "temper" the eggs (which means to bring up the temperature slowly so that the eggs don't scramble). Repeat with another one-third of the milk while continuing to whisk.

14. Cook the custard: Add the egg mixture to the pot containing the remainder of the milk and whisk to combine. Over medium heat, cook the mixture until it reaches 185°F (85°C) on a digital thermometer while continuing to whisk, making sure there are no lumps. Remove from the heat.

15. Melt the chocolate: Place the chopped chocolate in a large heatproof bowl. Pour the hot custard mixture over it. Let sit for a few minutes so the chocolate begins to melt. Using an immersion blender, blend until smooth.

16. In a small bowl, stir together the water and cocoa powder. Pour into the chocolate ganache mixture and blend until smooth.

17. Fill the pie and chill: Immediately fill the fully cooled pie shell with your just-made chocolate ganache (which will still be liquidy at this point, but will finish setting in the fridge). Transfer to the refrigerator to chill until the chocolate ganache sets (it'll be jiggly in texture and no longer a liquid), a few hours or up to overnight.

recipe continues

MEANWHILE, MAKE THE VANILLA WHIPPED CREAM

18. In a stand mixer fitted with the whisk (or a large bowl with a hand mixer or whisk), combine the heavy cream, sugar, and vanilla seeds (or extract). Whip on high speed until soft peaks form, just a few minutes. Refrigerate until ready to assemble the pie.

FINISH ASSEMBLING THE PIE

19. Remove the chilled pie from the fridge. Using a rubber spatula, spread a generous amount of vanilla whipped cream on top. Finish with a dusting of cocoa powder or chocolate shavings. Slice and serve right away.

STORAGE

Best enjoyed immediately. To store, cover tightly with plastic wrap and keep in the refrigerator for 1 to 2 days.

YOUR TURN TO COOK
CHERRY CLAFOUTIS

ONE OF THE downsides to being a professional chef is that you are *never* "not the chef." Ask any chef friend, and they'll tell you that when there's a meal being cooked—even if it is not in their own restaurant—they eventually wind up in the kitchen.

But one day, almost a decade ago now, I received an invite from Irene. Irene ran her own production company and created shows about some of the best chefs in the world and, of course, their food. Her Thanksgiving Eve parties were legendary feasts consisting of 93 pounds of pork butt, roasted until fork-tender with crackling skin; 500 ice-cold oysters; and unlimited drinks. She did it to give thanks to the chefs and food industry workers who would be cooking on actual Thanksgiving Day (in my case, making 2,000 pies). Irene became one of the few people who cooked for me, rather than the other way around.

The Thanksgiving Eve party at Irene's became a tradition for me and my family. Even in the years when we couldn't attend, Irene would pack up the meal and send it over to us for the whole team to share. It wasn't until recently that I realized I had never cooked for Irene.

Then the day came when I volunteered to resume my role as the chef rather than a diner. New York was just starting to warm up for the summer, the farmers' markets were filled with fresh sour cherries, and it didn't take long for Irene and me to get the same idea of what to make: a clafoutis. This subtly sweet tart with fresh fruits baked in custard until they lightly caramelize and just slightly burst is one of my favorites. Think of it as the best part of a pie but without the crust.

Irene watched as I prepared the fruits and measured out the ingredients. Clafoutis is all about the seasonal berries becoming little sugar bombs buried in the custard. My pick is sour cherries, which despite their name are as sweet as they are sour. They have a short season in the summer but add a distinctive tartness to the recipe. Eventually Irene couldn't resist jumping in to help. Standing next to me in the kitchen, she said, "Who says that one of us needs to cook for the other? Why can't we both cook together?" We decided to eat the clafoutis warm out of the oven, digging spoons directly into the pie pan. And standing up against the bar counter, mouths full, we decided that when among friends, there can never be too many chefs in the kitchen.

MAKES A 9-INCH (23 CM) CLAFOUTIS (SERVES 6 TO 8)

INGREDIENTS

Softened butter and flour, for the baking dish

39 grams	2 large	egg yolks
148 grams	3 large	eggs
246 grams	1¼ cups	sugar
49 grams	⅓ cup	all-purpose flour
5 grams	1¼ teaspoons	baking powder
246 grams	1 cup + 2 tablespoons	whole milk
246 grams	1 cup + 2 tablespoons	heavy cream

Vanilla seeds (scraped from ½ vanilla bean) or ¼ teaspoon vanilla extract

20 grams	4 teaspoons	kirsch (cherry brandy; optional)
450 grams	1 pound	pitted sweet or sour cherries* (I like Bing or Rainier cherries)

Whipped cream, for serving

* If fresh cherries aren't available, you can also use fresh blueberries or even sliced fresh apricots.

EQUIPMENT

9-inch (23 cm) round ceramic tart or pie dish or metal cake pan	Large bowl
	Whisk

1. Preheat the oven to 355°F (180°C).

2. Butter and flour the baking dish: Butter the base, sides, and inside edges of a 9-inch (23 cm) round baking dish or cake pan. Pour in some flour and shake it around until evenly coated. Tap out any excess.

3. Make the batter: In a large bowl, whisk together the egg yolks, whole eggs, and sugar until evenly combined. Add the flour and baking powder and stir until evenly combined. Add the milk, cream, and vanilla, stirring until combined. Stir in the kirsch (if using).

recipe continues

4. Assemble the clafoutis: Spread the cherries in an even layer in the bottom of the prepared pan. Pour the batter over the cherries until it reaches just under the top rim (this batter will not rise much).

5. Bake: Bake until the custard is just set and the edges are golden, and a paring knife poked into the center comes out clean, 40 to 55 minutes. The baking time will vary depending on how large/deep your baking dish is.

6. Let cool for 15 to 20 minutes, then serve warm with a dollop of whipped cream.

STORAGE

Best enjoyed fresh and while still warm. To store, cover tightly with plastic wrap and keep in the refrigerator for 1 to 2 days.

CRÊPES

ONE OF THE highest compliments that any chef can receive is that their food "tastes like home." Think about that climactic scene in the movie *Ratatouille* when the critic, after his first bite, mouth agape, is transported back to a moment in his childhood when he found unconditional love and comfort in a dish from his mom. To cook "like mom" is what we all strive to do.

Except in my case. My mom was a notoriously bad cook.

I grew up in a suburb on the north side of Paris. It wasn't the picturesque French countryside that most people imagine, but rather an industrial town that served as a hub for factory workers and their families. Food was one of the things that my parents never budgeted well for. Our meals came mostly out of cans and were often heated up to the point of unrecognizable dryness.

It wasn't long before I had to get my first job to help support the family. And it so happened the bakery owner also had an open position for my sister. I was doing an apprenticeship in the kitchen while my sister was positioned at a small crêpe station out in the front of the shop. That bakery was where we both got our start.

From that point on, our careers would go in very different directions. I ended up working every back-of-house position in a restaurant from porter to eventually pastry chef; the path took me across the world. And as for my sister? Twenty years later, I returned home and found her still working at the same bakery we started at.

I asked her if she felt like she had missed out on seeing the world, or wondered what life would have been like if she had done something else. And she only explained that nowhere else in the world felt the way home did. She was content and her family had grown. Life, though different for her, had been just as happy and fulfilling. To add to this, I have never seen anyone faster or more skilled at making crêpes than she is. She was right in many ways—home is the best place on earth.

So these days when I think of home, I think about the smell of the melting butter sizzling in a crêpe pan. I imagine the nuttiness of the batter as it crisps up on the sides. I think about her fast-moving hands busy at work.

And while I'm abroad and traveling or cooking with new friends, I always laugh at the saying that "the first crêpe is always wasted." I can't help but beg to differ that back at home, every crêpe my sister makes is perfect.

MAKES 15 TO 20 CRÊPES

INGREDIENTS

68 grams	⅓ cup	sugar
170 grams	3 large	eggs
4 grams	1½ teaspoons	salt
226 grams	1¾ cups	all-purpose flour
490 grams	2⅓ cups	whole milk
41 grams	3 tablespoons	unsalted butter, melted
A splash of rum (optional)		
Canola oil, for cooking		

Suggested Toppings

Lemons, for squeezing

Powdered sugar, brown sugar, honey

Jams

Butter

Chocolate or nut spreads

Fresh berries or bananas

EQUIPMENT

Large bowl	Small ladle
Whisk	Offset spatula
Crêpe pan or 10-inch nonstick skillet	

1. Make the crêpe batter: In a large bowl, whisk together the sugar, eggs, and salt. Add the flour and continue to whisk until it forms a paste (try to remove any lumps). Add the whole milk a little at a time and continue to whisk until you get a smooth liquid batter. Add the melted butter and whisk until combined. As an option you can add a little bit of rum for added flavor. (For best results, let the batter rest overnight or at least for 1 hour in the refrigerator.)

recipe continues

2. Cook the crêpes: Pour a tiny bit of canola oil into a crêpe pan or nonstick skillet set over medium-low heat and wipe it down with a paper towel, making sure there is no excess oil pooling in the pan. Use a ladle to pour a thin layer of the batter into the pan, rotating the pan so the batter forms a round that covers the entire base. The sides of the crêpe will slightly dry and crinkle inward as it cooks. Use an offset spatula to lightly separate the crêpe from the pan and push it inward. As the base of the crêpe cooks, it should move away from the pan easily in 1 to 2 minutes. Using the offset spatula, gently lift the crêpe and flip it over. Cook for an additional minute or so. Place the cooked crêpe on a large plate and continue to make more crêpes with the remaining batter.

3. Serve: Serve the crêpes immediately with your favorite toppings. (I love serving mine with honey or fresh berries. You can also dust them with powdered sugar, or a sprinkle of brown sugar with a squeeze of fresh lemon juice.)

STORAGE

Best enjoyed immediately.

THANK YOU
TEURGOULE

WHEN I FIRST moved to New York, almost fifteen years ago, I was warned that New Yorkers aren't friendly. In my apartment building, I would only ever hear my neighbors in the hallways outside but never meet them face-to-face. Indeed, even a decade after I moved in, I couldn't name a single person who lived in my building.

Then one day, there was a knock at the door. I found myself eye-to-eye with the new neighbor who lived down the hall. He explained that he and his family had just moved in and all their kitchen tools were stuck somewhere on a boat overseas. He was hoping for something that he could use to cook for his kids since they didn't really eat take-out food. At the end of his story, he asked if he could borrow any kind of equipment to bake some lasagna for the kids. I smiled. It was uncanny how he had knocked on the door of a chef. I quickly obliged and handed him a ceramic baking pan that I had on the stovetop. A few days later he returned with the pan in hand. Only it wasn't empty but filled with a frittata that he had made.

"A family recipe," he said. "It just didn't feel right to return it empty and not filled with food."

He was the first neighbor I ever became friends with. Over the next few years, we began a tradition of cooking for each other and our families. I would return a skillet a few days later with fudgy brownies that had the perfect crispy edges and molten center. He'd send back a Bolognese sauce cooked down over hours until it was rich and creamy. And so our cooking exchange continued for many years until I moved away. As a parting gift, I left the ceramic baking pan for him. My final recipe was for a French rice pudding called *teurgoule* that originated in Normandy. Rice, milk, cream, sugar, and cinnamon slowly bake down in the oven and form a dark skin on top that almost looks burnt until you scoop into the soft molten rice pudding underneath. The story goes that the smell of it baking was so intoxicating, folks couldn't wait to eat it, and when they spooned in piping-hot bites, they had to twist their mouths at how hot it was. Hence the name: *teurgoule* in old French means "twisted mouth."

A bit tongue-tied myself, I didn't actually say good-bye to my neighbor in person. There was no card, but I hope the message was clear. It was a thank-you for the friendship and for the food; two words that mean very much the same thing.

MAKES A 9-INCH (23 CM) OR 10-INCH (25 CM) TEURGOULE (SERVES 6 TO 8)

INGREDIENTS

1 kilogram	4¼ cups	whole milk
82 grams	½ cup	Arborio rice
82 grams	⅓ cup + 1 tablespoon	sugar
8 grams	1 tablespoon	rum

Vanilla seeds (scraped from 1 vanilla bean) or ½ teaspoon vanilla extract

Cinnamon, whipped cream, or ice cream, for serving

EQUIPMENT

Medium pot	9-inch (23 cm) or 10-inch (25 cm) cast-iron skillet or round ceramic baking dish
Silicone spatula	

1. Cook the rice: In a medium pot, combine the milk, rice, sugar, rum, and vanilla seeds (or extract) and bring to a boil over medium heat, stirring often with a silicone spatula to avoid burning or sticking on the bottom of the pot. Continue cooking, stirring often, until the rice is tender, about 30 minutes. Remove from the heat.

2. Meanwhile, preheat the oven to 355°F (180°C).

3. Bake the teurgoule: Pour the rice mixture into a 9-inch (23 cm) or 10-inch (25 cm) cast-iron skillet or round ceramic baking dish. Slide into the oven and bake until the rice pudding forms a thin skin that's deep golden in color and the center is no longer jiggly or wet: 1 hour to 1 hour 10 minutes in a cast-iron skillet; 15 to 20 minutes longer in a ceramic baking dish. The pudding will bubble up in the center during baking; don't worry, it will sink slightly once you remove it from the oven.

4. Remove from the oven and serve while still warm with a dusting of cinnamon, or with a dollop of freshly whipped cream or vanilla ice cream.

STORAGE

Best enjoyed immediately.

DARK CHOCOLATE BUDINO
WITH OLIVE OIL CHANTILLY

IN 2020, A few months after the pandemic started, food became more of a cure than it ever had been before. Amid the illness and fear, restaurants, bakeries, and cafés all around the world gathered together to make food for first responders. I remember dropping bags of baked goods off curbside at the hospitals with our gloved hands waving good-bye from behind the car window. Birthday gifts came in the form of food deliveries to your apartment.

That year, my son was born almost two months early and our lives became a series of daily trips, every three hours, to see him in the NICU, for thirty-nine days. We shared a small waiting room with other new parents and ate all our meals from the hospital menu. Every day, we would talk about how terrible the food was. That overcooked chicken breast, the unseasoned salmon. We'd all laugh at the shared disdain we had for the food. The only thing my wife ever finished on her plate was the chocolate pudding.

When she was pregnant with our second child, she had an intense battle with morning sickness. In an effort to help, I cooked most of our meals at home. One night for dessert, I served a quick chocolate treat. I chose good dark chocolate and slowly whisked it with heavy cream. A dollop of olive oil Chantilly cream was lightly whipped to add a slight tanginess and cut through the rich chocolate, and a sprinkling of sea salt gave it a new dimension. For many weeks following, she would ask for it. I have never told her that my inspiration was actually the hospital chocolate pudding.

MAKES 4 SERVINGS

INGREDIENTS

6 grams	2 teaspoons	unflavored gelatin powder
14 grams	1 tablespoon	water
774 grams	4 cups	heavy cream
33 grams	2 tablespoons + 2 teaspoons	sugar
155 grams	1½ cups	chopped dark chocolate (at least 60% cacao)

For Serving

Olive Oil Chantilly (recipe follows), well chilled*

Olive oil, for finishing

Sea salt, for finishing

I recommend you make the Chantilly the day before you plan to serve the pudding, but you don't have to. You can also make it a couple hours before.

EQUIPMENT

Small bowl	Large heatproof bowl
Whisk	Silicone spatula
Medium pot	Four 7-ounce ramekins/small bowls

1. Bloom the gelatin: In a small bowl, whisk together the gelatin and water until dissolved. Let the mixture sit a few minutes until the gelatin has bloomed (when it has absorbed the majority of the liquid, gaining 2 to 3 times its original volume, and feels firm and set).

2. Heat the cream: In a medium pot, combine the heavy cream and sugar and bring to a simmer over medium-high heat, stirring occasionally with a whisk (do not boil). Remove from the heat. Stir the gelatin mixture into the hot cream mixture until dissolved.

3. Melt the chocolate: Place the chopped chocolate in a large heatproof bowl. Pour the hot cream mixture over the chocolate. Let sit for a few minutes so that the chocolate starts to melt.

4. Gently stir with a silicone spatula or whisk until the chocolate is fully melted and the mixture is smooth.

5. Portion the mixture into four 7-ounce ramekins or bowls.

6. Chill the budinos: Cover each ramekin or bowl with plastic wrap. Refrigerate for a few hours, or up to overnight, until the pudding fully sets (it should no longer be a liquid). Keep chilled until ready to serve.

7. To serve: Add a dollop of the Chantilly to each chilled pudding and finish with a drizzle of olive oil and a sprinkling of sea salt. Extra Chantilly is a great dip for fruit or topping for hot chocolate or coffee.

STORAGE

Best enjoyed immediately. To store, cover tightly with plastic wrap and keep in the refrigerator for 2 to 3 days.

OLIVE OIL CHANTILLY

INGREDIENTS

3 grams	1 teaspoon	unflavored gelatin powder
17 grams	1 tablespoon + 2 teaspoons	water
160 grams	¾ cup	heavy cream #1
39 grams	3 tablespoons	sugar
Vanilla seeds (scraped from 1 vanilla bean) or ½ teaspoon vanilla extract		
91 grams	½ cup	mascarpone
160 grams	¾ cup	heavy cream #2
40 grams	¼ cup	extra-virgin olive oil

recipe continues

EQUIPMENT

Small bowl	Immersion blender
Whisk	Stand mixer (or hand mixer)
Medium pot	

1. Bloom the gelatin: In a small bowl, whisk together the gelatin and water until dissolved. Let the mixture sit a few minutes until the gelatin has bloomed.

2. Heat the cream: In a medium pot, combine heavy cream #1 (¾ cup/160 g) and the sugar and bring to a simmer over medium heat, stirring occasionally with a whisk until the sugar is dissolved. Do not boil.

3. Stir in the gelatin mixture and vanilla seeds (or extract) until combined. Remove from the heat.

4. Blend the mascarpone and cream: Place the mascarpone in a large bowl. Carefully pour the hot cream mixture over the mascarpone and use an immersion blender to blend until smooth. Pour in heavy cream #2 (¾ cup/160 g) and the olive oil and blend until smooth.

5. Chill the Chantilly cream: Cover the Chantilly in plastic wrap that touches the surface to prevent a skin from forming. Refrigerate until set (the texture should be very thick and jiggly, and no longer a liquid), a few hours or up to overnight. Keep chilled until ready to serve. This Chantilly recipe should be made the day before, so it's fully set and chilled.

6. Whip the Chantilly: When ready to serve, in a stand mixer fitted with the whisk (or in a large bowl with a hand mixer), whip the chilled Chantilly* until light and fluffy medium peaks form.

Make sure your Chantilly is cold. If it's room temperature or warm, it won't whip up into fluffy peaks.

STORAGE

To store, cover with plastic wrap that touches the surface (to prevent a skin from forming) and keep in the refrigerator for 2 to 3 days.

YOU'VE EARNED IT

BRIOCHE LOAF

WHEN MAY ROLLS around, graduation gowns flow through the streets, and our SoHo neighborhood feels like a college town. Weeks before, we would have seen the same students, sans their graduation gowns, grabbing their fourth cup of coffee and a cookie pick-me-up prior to final exams. After they survived the heat, they emerged "fully cooked."

One graduation season, a guest in line stopped me. She explained that four years ago, she had written her college application essay about the bakery. And now she was graduating from the school of her dreams. The only thing she hadn't done was bake.

"My college essay was about visiting the bakery and mixing together the right ingredients with creativity," she said, as if quoting her own lines. "But I've only ever been a spectator in a kitchen, never a chef."

We decided that for her to truly come full circle, she would need to try her hand at making something. I assigned her a brioche recipe as it was the final recipe I had to execute when I graduated from my apprenticeship at culinary school. A brioche is our "daily bread" in France, and is a buttery, eggy bread that is almost yellow in color from the richness. Simply toasted and eaten with some butter or jam makes for a satisfying breakfast. Back in the old days, we culinary students executed everything by hand and recited the recipe by memory. It was physical; it took speed and focus. In my class of twelve, I finished first with 17 points out of 20; the next one who passed scored 11 points; and only one more person passed, at 10.5 points. The other nine people failed and had to repeat the entire year.

She looked at me as if I had just given her a pop quiz. When she left that day, I thought maybe I wouldn't hear from her again, but almost a year later, we received an email in our info inbox. It was a picture of her with a brioche. Golden, well-shaped, and perfectly worthy of graduating with honors.

MAKES 1 LOAF, PLUS ABOUT 5 BUNS

INGREDIENTS

Brioche Dough

407 grams	3¼ cups	all-purpose flour
10 grams	1 tablespoon + 1 teaspoon	kosher salt
50 grams	¼ cup	sugar
6 grams	2 teaspoons	active dry yeast
264 grams	5 large	eggs
20 grams	4 teaspoons	whole milk
227 grams	2 sticks (8 oz)	unsalted butter, at room temperature and very soft

Egg Wash

50 grams	1 large	egg
5 grams	1 teaspoon	whole milk
1 gram	¼ teaspoon	salt

EQUIPMENT

Stand mixer with a dough hook	Small bowl
Sheet pan	Whisk
Kitchen scale	Pastry brush
8½ × 4½-inch (11 × 21.5 cm) metal loaf pan	

MAKE THE BRIOCHE DOUGH

1. Mix the dry ingredients: In a stand mixer fitted with the dough hook, combine the flour, salt, sugar, and yeast and mix on low speed until evenly combined.

2. Add the eggs: Add the eggs in one at a time, mixing on high speed until each egg is incorporated before adding the next. Your dough will start to form and develop elasticity.

3. Add the milk: Add the milk all at once and mix on high speed until fully incorporated. Now it's time to work the dough, scraping the sides of the bowl periodically in between mixing on high speed until the dough pulls away from the sides. The dough should be slightly warm to the touch.

4. Add the butter: Add the softened butter and continue to mix still on high until all the butter is fully incorporated, 10 to 12 minutes. Eventually the dough will pull off the sides of the mixer and become smooth.

5. First fermentation/proof: Line a sheet pan with plastic wrap and transfer the dough to the pan. Loosely wrap the dough with the plastic wrap. Now it's time for the first fermentation or "proofing." Leave the dough out in a slightly warmer than room temperature space (ideally 82°F/28°C)* with some humidity (i.e., near an oven) to proof until it doubles in size, 1 to 1½ hours.

6. Chill the dough: Once proofed, remove the plastic and use the palms of your hands to push down the dough to degas it, or rid it of air. Rewrap the dough in plastic and place it in the refrigerator to chill for 1 to 1½ hours.

  * *If your house isn't that warm inside, you can proof the dough inside the cold oven with the oven light on.*

7. Second fermentation/proof: Remove the dough from the refrigerator and once again degas it by pressing down with the palm of your hands. Rewrap the dough in plastic and return it to the refrigerator to rest for at least a few hours, but preferably overnight.

8. Portion the dough: Lightly flour a flat work surface. Using a scale, weigh out 750 grams of dough.*

  * *You'll have almost 250 grams dough left over. Roll it into about 5 small buns for sandwiches or dinner rolls, which should be baked right after they are shaped and proofed, or frozen after they are shaped (although baked right away yields better results).*

9. Shape the loaf: Gently shape the dough with your hands into a rectangle that's about 8 × 12 inches (20 × 30 cm). Form the dough into a loaf shape by bringing the top down toward you one-third of the way, then bringing the bot-

recipe continues

tom up one-third of the way (like you're folding a letter in thirds). Carefully flip the loaf over so the seam is now at the bottom. Place the loaf, seam side down, into an 8½ × 4½-inch (11 × 21.5 cm) metal loaf pan.

10. Proof: Allow the dough to proof in the loaf pan in a warm area slightly above room temperature until it has doubled in size, 2 to 2½ hours. Once the dough has come up a bit over the top of the loaf pan, it's ready to bake. (Check every 30 minutes or so, so the dough doesn't overproof. Depending on the temperature and humidity in your space, your dough may proof faster or slower.)

11. Position a rack in the center of the oven and preheat the oven to 350°F (175°C). Do this at the 1½-hour mark of proofing so the loaf can go right in the oven when it is fully proofed.

MAKE THE EGG WASH

12. In a small bowl, whisk together the egg, milk, and salt. With a pastry brush, lightly egg wash the surface of the loaf, making sure not to deflate the dough.

13. Bake: Bake the loaf until golden brown on top, 35 to 40 minutes.

14. Unmold: Once out of the oven, let cool slightly but unmold while still warm. Serve immediately.

STORAGE

Best enjoyed right away. To store, cover with plastic wrap or place in an airtight container. If you are storing it for longer than 1 day, keep it at room temperature (unrefrigerated) and refresh by reheating in the oven at 350°F (175°C), or slice and toast.

NUTELLA MILK BREAD

DURING THE SUMMERTIME, a large number of interns line up at the bakery. It is a rite of passage for them to stand in line, young, eager, and dressed in their business casual attire, to secure a breakfast order for their bosses. They are easy to spot at the cash register. There's usually a list of orders on their phone that they're always double-checking, and they are always in a rush. You sense a different vibe when ordering breakfast is for work rather than pleasure.

A few summers ago, there was one particularly hardworking intern who was always first in line every weekday morning. Our team affectionately referred to her as "the Best Intern," since even in scorching hot weather or a drenching rainstorm, she would always cheerfully walk in and greet our team. At the end of her order, she'd always throw in a Nutella Milk Bread for herself. Something about the soft brioche dough with crispy hazelnuts and chocolate gave her the fuel she needed for the day ahead. She let us know that she was hoping to perform well over the summer and be given an offer for a full-time position when she graduated. By the end of summer, our whole team was rooting for her.

"Today's the last day of my internship," she announced one August morning. Her performance review was that afternoon, and we wished her good luck as she masterfully juggled the different bags of *viennoiserie* and trays of coffee in both hands and gestured good-bye with her elbow.

It wasn't until the following year that "the Intern" returned to the shop. She had a new haircut and was now sporting a blazer, but we instantly recognized her. She proudly announced she had in fact scored that dream job and this was her first day at work. Her days of waiting in line were over, she said. But since it was her first day back, she wanted to honor the tradition by getting a few things for her team, including her regular order of Nutella Milk Bread for herself.

That was the last time we saw her, but every time an intern waits in line and Nutella Milk Bread is a part of their order, I wonder if it's for her, now as the boss instead of the intern, but faithfully a pastry lover to the end.

MAKES 20 TO 24 NUTELLA MILK BREADS

INGREDIENTS

Brioche Dough

2 kilograms	double recipe	Brioche Dough (page 34)

Nutella Pastry Cream

429 grams	2 cups	whole milk
51 grams	¼ cup	sugar #1
51 grams	¼ cup	sugar #2
50 grams	¼ cup	cornstarch
128 grams	6 large	egg yolks
253 grams	1 cup	Nutella
42 grams	6 tablespoons	unsweetened cocoa powder, sifted (I like to use Dutch-process)

For Baking

100 grams	2 large	eggs
10 grams	2 teaspoons	whole milk
2 grams	½ teaspoon	salt
25 grams	¼ cup	roughly chopped hazelnuts

EQUIPMENT

Medium pot	Offset spatula
Small bowl	Baking sheets
Whisk	Sharp knife
Silicone spatula	Silicone baking mat or parchment paper
Rolling pin	Pastry brush

recipe continues

MAKE THE BRIOCHE DOUGH (DAY BEFORE)

1. Make the brioche dough as directed through the second fermentation (step 7) and refrigerate overnight.

MAKE THE NUTELLA PASTRY CREAM (DAY BEFORE OR DAY OF)

2. Warm the milk: In a medium pot, bring the milk and sugar #1 (¼ cup/51 g) to a boil, continuously stirring with a whisk. Remove from the heat.

3. Temper the eggs: In a small bowl, whisk together sugar #2 (¼ cup/51 g) with the cornstarch. Add the egg yolks, one at a time, whisking until combined. Slowly pour one-third of the hot milk mixture into the yolk mixture. Whisk until evenly combined. Add another one-third of the milk mixture, whisking until combined. Pour the warmed eggs back into the pot of the remaining milk.*

* This process is called tempering, which is a cooking technique in which you gradually raise the temperature of a cold or room-temperature ingredient (in this case, the egg yolk mixture) by adding small amounts of a hot liquid, to prevent the cold ingredient from cooking too quickly or too much. If you add all of the hot liquid into the egg yolks at once, you're going to end up with lumpy scrambled eggs in your pastry cream.

4. Over low to medium heat, while stirring constantly with a silicone spatula, heat the mixture until it noticeably thickens. It takes about 5 or so minutes, with the thickening coming in the last 2 minutes. It will continue to thicken as it cools, so remove it from the heat before too much water evaporates.

5. Fold in the Nutella: Fold in the Nutella and cocoa powder with a silicone spatula, until evenly combined. A good pastry cream is rich and smooth, with a glossy and velvety texture.*

* If you notice any lumps, strain the pastry cream through a fine-mesh sieve or use an immersion blender to help smooth out the texture.

6. Chill the pastry cream: Cover with plastic wrap directly pressed onto the surface of the pastry cream and let it fully cool in the fridge, a few hours (or up to overnight). When you're ready to assemble the milk bread, temper the pastry cream by bringing it out of the fridge and stirring it with a rubber spatula to make it smooth and spreadable.

7. Shape the milk bread: Remove the dough from the fridge and transfer it to a well-floured work surface. Using a rolling pin, roll it out into a rectangle that is roughly 23 × 16 inches (58 × 40 cm) and ¼ inch (6 mm) thick. Set the rectangle with a long side facing you. With an offset spatula, spread the cooled Nutella pastry cream over the top of the dough. Leave a bare border all around so that the cream doesn't ooze out. Roll the dough up tightly from the bottom with your fingertips to form a log that's about 23½ inches (60 cm) long and 2½ inches (6.5 cm) in diameter.

8. Chill the log: Place the log onto a baking sheet lined with parchment paper (you can use a bench knife to help you move the dough). If the dough starts to feel warm and very soft, chill the log in the refrigerator for 1 hour.

9. Cut into rolls: Remove the log of dough from the fridge, reshaping it as necessary to get it back to 23½ inches (60 cm) long. Use a sharp knife to cut alternating diagonal cuts to form trapezoid-shaped rolls that are 3 to 3½ inches (7.5 to 9 cm) wide on the wider side and about 100 grams each, cleaning the knife between the cuts (so the Nutella filling doesn't smear). You'll get 20 to 24 trapezoid-shaped rolls.

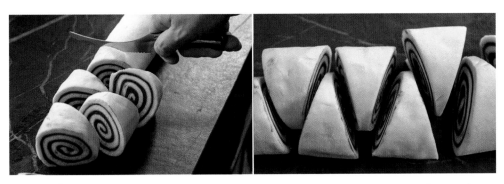

recipe continues

10. Proof the rolls: Line a baking sheet with a silicone baking mat or parchment paper. Set the rolls on the lined sheet 2 to 2½ inches (5 to 6.5 cm) apart, with the cut sides on the left and right, and the seams tucked into the bottom. Use your index finger and gently press down on the middle of the rolls to slightly flatten them. Proof the rolls in a warm area slightly above room temperature until they double in size, 1½ to 2 hours.

BAKE THE MILK BREAD (DAY OF)

11. Preheat the oven to 355°F (180°C).

12. In a small bowl, combine the eggs, milk, and salt with a whisk to make an egg wash. Using a pastry brush, gently brush a thin even layer of egg wash over the rolls on the top and sides.

13. Sprinkle the chopped hazelnuts over the tops.

14. Bake until golden brown, 10 to 12 minutes.

15. Let cool for a few minutes and enjoy while they're still warm.

STORAGE

Best enjoyed right away. To store, cover with plastic wrap or place in an airtight container and keep at room temperature for up to 1 day.

CHAPTER 2
The Friendship Years

There are moments in all our lives when our friends are our community, and cooking becomes a group effort. Whether for potlucks or game nights or surprise parties, our friends can be our favorite people to bake for and feed.

HAZELNUT CAKE

ONE COLD WINTER, we decided to make a wishing tree. I had first seen wishing trees during Tanabata (the Star Festival) in Japan, where the tradition is to write your wish on a strip of paper and tie it to the branches of a tree with the hopes that it will come true. The bare branches soon become lush and full of multicolored paper-strip "leaves." Like candy-colored weeping willows, the trees rustle in the wind, as if they are whispering the wishes they carry. And in New York during February, after four bleak and cold months, we could all use some wishful thinking for better times ahead.

I gathered a few large branches from the park and secured them in a pot of rocks. Next to it, I laid out strips of colored paper and pens. The instructions were simple: make a wish and tie it onto the branch.

As the days passed, the branches filled up with paper wishes. Until one day, my wife asked me: "What do we do with the wishes? It doesn't feel right to just throw them away."

The night after Valentine's Day, we took down the wishing tree and carefully removed each of the paper strips. It was fascinating to see what everyone had wished for. From getting the job they interviewed for to passing an exam to saving up enough money for an apartment to babies to a proposal that ends with a yes. There they were—life's different milestones.

"I hope they all got their wishes," I remember saying. And a part of me wondered if they would return to the bakery to celebrate their accomplishments with a sweet treat. I looked up to see my wife smiling.

"You'll enjoy this one," she said, handing me a single strip of paper. On it, in neatly printed letters, was a different type of wish. It simply said: "A gluten-free hazelnut cake, please."

I imagined that whoever had written this may have not had many options for dessert as they are often not gluten-free. And so when developing spring recipes, I pulled together my thoughts and created a nutty hazelnut cake that didn't require flour. The ingredients were simple, but they made an intoxicating cake that was moist and both satisfying and light at the same time. I put it on the bakery menu when March rolled around. It was the one wish I had the power to grant.

MAKES AN 8-INCH (20 CM) CAKE (SERVES 4 TO 6)

INGREDIENTS

64 grams	¼ cup + 2 teaspoons	granulated sugar #1
92 grams	5 large	egg yolks
138 grams	5 large	egg whites
64 grams	¼ cup + 2 teaspoons	granulated sugar #2
121 grams	1½ cups	hazelnut flour
30 grams	3 tablespoons + 1 teaspoon	cornstarch
Softened unsalted butter, for the pan		
Hazelnut flour, for the pan		
23 grams	¼ cup	chopped hazelnuts
Powdered sugar, for finishing		

For Serving

Fresh ricotta

Honeycomb

Grated orange zest

EQUIPMENT

Stand mixer	Pastry brush
Mixing bowl	8-inch (20 cm) round cake pan
Rubber spatula	

1. Position a rack in the center of the oven and preheat the oven to 355°F (180°C).

2. Whisk the yolks: In a stand mixer fitted with the whisk, whisk sugar #1 (¼ cup + 2 teaspoons/64 g) and the yolks together on high speed until the mixture is light and fluffy, 2 to 3 minutes. Transfer to a separate bowl. Wash and fully dry the stand mixer bowl and whisk attachment.

3. Whip the egg whites: In the washed and dried stand mixer bowl fitted with the whisk, whisk the egg whites on high speed until they're foamy, 1 to 2 minutes.

Gradually add sugar #2 (¼ cup + 2 teaspoons/64 g), while continuing to mix on high speed, until stiff peaks form.

4. Fold the yolks into the whites: Using a rubber spatula, carefully fold one-third of the yolk mixture into the egg whites. Repeat with two more additions, folding together after each one, until the two are just combined. Do not overmix or the mixture will deflate.

5. Stir in the hazelnut flour: Slowly add the hazelnut flour in three additions, folding with a spatula until just combined. Fold in the cornstarch until just combined. Do not overmix (the weight of the hazelnut flour can deflate the fluffy batter if added too quickly or overmixed).

6. Butter and flour the cake pan: Using a pastry brush (or your hands), brush a thin layer of softened butter into an 8-inch (20 cm) round cake pan, making sure to get into the edge and up the sides of the pan. Pour a handful of hazelnut flour into the buttered pan and toss it around to coat the inside, then tap out any excess.

7. Bake the cake: Pour the batter into the prepared pan. Sprinkle the chopped hazelnuts evenly across the top.

8. Bake until lightly golden brown and a cake tester or paring knife inserted into the center comes out clean, about 30 minutes.

9. Let cool in the pan for 10 to 15 minutes. Place a plate or platter over the top of the pan, and carefully invert to unmold the cake. Turn the cake over so the chopped hazelnuts are on the top.

10. Finish with a dusting of powdered sugar and serve with a dollop of fresh ricotta, honeycomb, and a bit of orange zest.

STORAGE

Best enjoyed as soon as possible. To store, cover with plastic wrap and keep at room temperature for 2 to 3 days.

LEMON BUNDT CAKE WITH
LIMONCELLO SYRUP

WHEN YOU LIVE in a city like New York, the weather sets the tone for everyone's mood. On the first warm day of spring, you're greeted by friendly neighbors, excited guests, and smiles. The rain, on the other hand, can bring on quite the opposite scenario.

On rainy days, our guests are usually less patient and more challenging; the interactions are short and somber. But during a particularly bad downpour one afternoon, we met a photographer who was giddily splashing through puddles on the street. Eventually, he came inside the bakery to dry off and drink a warm cup of coffee. I remember asking him what he was photographing and being surprised when he answered: "The rain."

It turns out, he had been photographing thunderstorms for several years all around the world. At first, I wondered why he would want to capture such a dreary day when the city looks so much better with a blue-sky backdrop. He could tell by my furrowed brow that I was confused.

"What I like to do is hang the photos up around my house," he said, "because rainy days are the best days to stay home."

How this tiny change in perspective made the rain so beautiful! In avoiding the rain, we learn to appreciate the comfort of resting at home. A few days later the photographer returned and got his usual cup of coffee. He bid a quick farewell to our cashier and said that he was leaving New York. And as he was headed out the door, I blurted out one final question: "What do you do on rainy days at home? You don't feel bored or stuck indoors?"

He smiled and answered without hesitation: "On those days, I bake. Like you, chef."

These days, I seldom bake at home since I spend 90 percent of my time baking in the kitchens at the bakery. But occasionally, I will make something—and usually when I do, it's raining outside. When life gives you lemons, make lemon cake. This particular one involves drenching your cake in a fragrant syrup of lemon juice and limoncello.

MAKES A 10-INCH (25 CM) BUNDT CAKE (SERVES 8 TO 10)

INGREDIENTS

Lemon Bundt Cake

250 grams	2 sticks + 3 tablespoons (9½ oz)	unsalted butter, at room temperature
400 grams	2 cups	granulated sugar
300 grams	6 large	eggs
180 grams	⅔ cup + 2 teaspoons	whole milk

Vanilla seeds (scraped from 1 vanilla bean) or ½ teaspoon vanilla extract

15 grams	2 tablespoons	grated lemon zest (from 5 to 6 lemons)
500 grams	3½ cups	all-purpose flour
15 grams	4 teaspoons	baking powder
200 grams	1 cup	lemon juice (from 6 to 8 lemons)

Softened unsalted butter and all-purpose flour, for the pan

Limoncello Syrup

100 grams	½ cup	lemon juice (from 3 to 4 lemons)
200 grams	1 cup	water
200 grams	1 cup	granulated sugar
47 grams	¼ cup	limoncello (Italian lemon liqueur)

For Finishing

Powdered sugar, for dusting

EQUIPMENT

Stand mixer (or hand mixer)	Medium pot
Citrus zester or grater	Sheet pan
Large bowl	Wire cooling rack
Whisk	Pastry brush
12-cup (10 inch/25 cm) Bundt pan	

MAKE THE LEMON BUNDT CAKE

1. Position a rack in the center of the oven and preheat the oven to 320°F (160°C).

2. Cream the butter and sugar: In a stand mixer fitted with the paddle (or in a large bowl with a hand mixer), cream the butter and granulated sugar together on medium speed until the mixture looks light and pale, 2 to 3 minutes.

3. Beat in the eggs and milk: Add the eggs one at a time while continuing to mix, waiting for each egg to be fully incorporated into the batter before adding the next. Add the milk, vanilla seeds (or extract), and lemon zest and mix until combined.

4. Add the flour: In a large bowl, whisk together the flour and baking powder. Gradually add the flour mixture into the batter in three additions, mixing until incorporated after each one, stopping to scrape down the sides of the bowl as needed. Add the lemon juice. Continue to mix until combined and there are no lumps in the batter.

5. Butter and flour the pan: Butter the inside of a 12-cup (10 inch/25 cm) pan first, making sure to get all the way up the sides and into any creases. Pour in a handful of flour and shake it around until the pan is evenly coated, then tap out any excess.

6. Bake the cake: Pour the batter into the mold until it's three-quarters of the way full (the cake will rise when baking). Place the pan on a baking sheet.

7. Bake until golden blond and a paring knife/cake tester inserted in the cake comes out clean, 1 hour 15 minutes to 1 hour 25 minutes.

MEANWHILE, MAKE THE LIMONCELLO SYRUP

8. In a medium pot, combine the lemon juice, water, granulated sugar, and limoncello and bring to a boil over high heat, stirring occasionally with a whisk. Remove from the heat and let cool for 15 to 20 minutes.

recipe continues

TO FINISH

9. Brush on the syrup: Let the Bundt cake cool in the pan for 10 to 15 minutes before inverting and unmolding the cake onto a wire rack set over a sheet pan. Pour a generous amount of the limoncello syrup over the cake (make sure both the syrup and the cake are warm, which will help the syrup absorb better), using a pastry brush to brush on more as needed and letting the syrup absorb fully before adding any more (you'll likely use half to three-quarters of the total amount of syrup).

10. Let cool for 10 to 15 minutes. Dust the cake with powdered sugar, then slice and serve.

STORAGE

Best enjoyed fresh and while still warm. To store, cover tightly with plastic wrap or place in an airtight container and keep in a cool dry place for up to 2 days.

HOMEMADE CHERRY MACADAMIA GRANOLA

DURING MY EARLY days in New York working for Restaurant Daniel, dinnertime at home landed around two in the morning. The sad truth for pastry chefs working in restaurants is that they are always the last ones dismissed, since dessert is the last course. By the time I got home, the options were slim for 24-hour restaurants that delivered. And so, my go-to meal of choice was simple: a bowl of cereal. Cereal was convenient. There was no prep time, there were minimal dishes to be washed, and it strangely hit the spot.

Most folks assume that a chef's dining calendar is filled with the city's hottest restaurants and glorious multicourse tastings. But there I would be, sitting on the couch, trying to crunch softly on cornflakes so I didn't wake up my wife. Inevitably she would hear me rustling around the kitchen and come out of our bedroom. We'd talk about the day as she rubbed the sleep out of her eyes. And I'd stretch out my back, which was sore from hours of standing in the kitchen. And then as I got ready for bed, she'd slowly start getting ready for the day. My very late dinner and her way-too-early breakfast was a brief moment when our schedules crossed. It wasn't glamorous, but it was precious.

These days my schedule has improved, now that I no longer work in a full-service restaurant. I try to get home at a decent hour to have dinner with the kids. But I still have a soft spot in my heart for cereal as an ingredient. Whether adding some chocolate for a decadent snack or sprinkling on some spice and salt for the holidays, a little bit of creativity turns the everyday item into something special. My favorite combination involves salted macadamia nuts and dried cherries. The first time I made this granola, after dinner, cleanup, and putting our kids to bed, my wife and I sat on the couch and had a small bowl each. It felt familiar sitting there, exhaling from a day of work. I asked her how it tasted, to which she responded: "Like the good ole days."

MAKES ABOUT 4 CUPS (1 KG)

INGREDIENTS

91 grams	½ cup	roughly chopped macadamia nuts
104 grams	1 cup	sliced almonds
196 grams	1 stick + 6 tablespoons (7 oz)	unsalted butter, at room temperature
196 grams	1 cup packed	dark brown sugar
261 grams	3 cups	old-fashioned rolled oats
76 grams	½ cup	golden raisins
76 grams	½ cup	dried cherries

EQUIPMENT

Sheet pan	Stand mixer (or hand mixer)
Parchment paper	Spatula
Small bowl	Silicone baking mat

1. Position a rack in the center of the oven and preheat the oven to 350°F (180°C). Line a sheet pan with parchment paper.

2. Toast the macadamia nuts and almonds: Spread the nuts on the lined pan and toast until lightly golden in color, 10 to 15 minutes (be careful not to over-toast the macadamias; they have a higher level of fat content than most nuts, so they tend to burn more easily). Transfer the nuts to a small bowl and set aside. Leave the oven on.

3. Cream the butter and sugar: In a stand mixer fitted with the paddle (or in a large bowl with a hand mixer), cream together the butter and brown sugar on medium speed until the mixture is combined and light and fluffy, 2 to 3 minutes.

4. Add the oats and mix until just combined.

5. Bake the granola: Using your hands or a spatula, evenly spread the granola mixture onto the lined baking sheet that was used to toast the nuts. Bake until the granola is lightly golden in color, 10 to 12 minutes.

6. Remove from the oven and break up any large pieces with a spatula or bench scraper (be careful as the granola will be very hot). Gently toss the granola using a spatula and evenly redistribute it on the baking sheet, then return it to the oven to bake until golden brown, an additional 3 to 5 minutes.

7. Remove from the oven. Check for any large pieces to break up as needed. Let cool for 20 to 30 minutes.

8. Toss in the nuts and fruit: Add the macadamia nuts, almonds, raisins, and dried cherries and toss with a spatula until everything is well distributed. Enjoy with your morning yogurt, sprinkled on top of ice cream, or just by the handful!

STORAGE

To store, place in an airtight container and keep in a cool dry place for up to 4 weeks.

APPLE TARTE TATIN

WE ALL HAVE that one friend. The one who shows up unannounced, rarely plans ahead, and somehow ends up on top. Mine is named Will, and he is especially spontaneous in the realm of food. When Will invites you over for a dinner party, the menu is never set. If the thought of hosting a large group of people with nothing prepared gives you anxiety, I'm with you. But Will delights in the assembling of his little "mystery box": some stone fruits he saw that day in the farmers' market or a tomato sauce he had lying around.

Maybe he thinks that's fun and that it livens up the party. Or perhaps he simply doesn't remember to buy supplies earlier. Either way, it always causes me stress. A pastry chef is perhaps the most type A personality in the kitchen. Every recipe is measured, every component of mise en place prepared in advance. And the reflex response from a chef whenever there's a group of people waiting for food is to start cooking.

So there I was at yet another spur-of-the-moment group dinner, rolling up my sleeves and trying to make something out of the box filled with shrimp, tomatoes, and bread. Eventually I shaped it into a panzanella salad for one course and shrimp toast for another. By the end of the meal, I couldn't help but ask Will why he wouldn't want to prepare the menu beforehand. After all, remember that one time when everyone went hungry?

That's when Will explained to me that he believed in "happy accidents." "Some of the best dishes in history are invented when something goes wrong," he explained. "Someone doesn't heat up their oven enough and the chocolate lava cake is born. You accidently drop some chocolate pieces into a recipe, and it turns into chocolate chip cookies. It's important to leave room for mistakes."

I looked in his box and saw apples. Immediately I thought of what I would make with some good butter and a splash of the apple brandy I knew Will had a stash of. One of my go-to recipes is the tarte tatin, a classic dessert supposedly invented when the Tatin sisters accidently dropped their apple tart on the floor. And I have done many variations of it, but they all involve at their core the slow cooking down of large wedges of apples until they are dark amber and then baking them with a buttery puff pastry. The puff pastry in the recipe is an important costar with the apples, adding a flakiness and a buttery base for the dripping caramel.

There are two kinds of puff pastry: When the butter is on the *inside*, it's a *regular* puff pastry. When the butter is on the *outside*—like this one—it's a *reversed* (or *inverse*) puff pastry, which can result in a flakier and more caramelized pastry, and it's my preference. It takes at least a day to make, but sometimes you can cheat (or "improvise" as Will likes to call it) and grab some frozen puff pastry at a local grocery store.

"What's for dessert?" Will asked. And on cue, I answered, "It's your favorite: a surprise."

MAKES AN 8-INCH (20 CM) TARTE TATIN (SERVES 6 TO 8)

INGREDIENTS

Reversed Puff Pastry Dough*

350 grams	2¾ cups	all-purpose flour
9 grams	1½ teaspoons	salt
150 grams	½ cup + 2 tablespoons	cold water
113 grams	1 stick (4 oz)	unsalted butter, at room temperature

All-purpose flour, for dusting

> *You can also use store-bought puff pastry instead, but I always prefer to make my own! If you're using store-bought puff pastry, skip to the Caramelized Apples step.*

Butter Block for Puff Pastry

127 grams	1 cup	all-purpose flour
253 grams	2 sticks + 2 tablespoons (9 oz)	unsalted butter, at room temperature

Caramelized Apples

265 grams	2⅓ cups	sugar
77 grams	5 tablespoons (2½ oz)	unsalted butter, at room temperature

6 to 8 apples (Honeycrisp or Gala), peeled, cored, and halved

For Serving

Crème fraîche or vanilla ice cream

EQUIPMENT

Stand mixer with a dough hook	Baking sheet
Parchment paper	Paring knife
Ruler	8-inch (20 cm) round cake pan
Pencil	Medium saucepan
Large offset spatula	Silicone spatula
Rolling pin	Silicone baking mat

MAKE THE REVERSED PUFF PASTRY DOUGH (DAY BEFORE)

1. Mix the dough: In a stand mixer fitted with the dough hook, combine the flour, salt, cold water, and butter. Mix on low speed until just blended, about 2½ minutes. The dough should look rough (since there's been no gluten development at this stage just yet).

2. Chill the dough: Dust a work surface with flour. With your hands, shape the dough into a square that's about ⅜ inch (1 cm) thick. Cover with plastic wrap and refrigerate until chilled, about 45 minutes. Wash and fully dry the stand mixer bowl.

MAKE THE BUTTER BLOCK (DAY BEFORE)

3. Blend the flour and butter: In a stand mixer fitted with the paddle, combine the all-purpose flour and butter and mix on low speed, stopping to scrape down the sides and bottom of the bowl as needed, until there are no streaks of butter. The mixture should feel like soft and pliable butter.

4. Chill the butter block: On a piece of parchment paper, use a ruler and pencil to draw a square that's just a bit under twice the length and width of your dough square. Flip the parchment paper over so the butter won't come into contact with the pencil marks. Place the butter in the center of the square and spread evenly with an offset spatula to fill the square. Refrigerate for 20 minutes, until firm but still pliable.

recipe continues

5. Remove the butter from the fridge: The butter should still be soft enough to bend slightly without cracking. (If it's too firm, lightly beat the butter with a rolling pin on a lightly floured surface until it becomes pliable. Make sure to press the butter back into its original square shape.)

6. Remove the dough from the fridge: Unwrap the chilled dough square and place in the center of the butter block so it looks like a diamond in the center of the square (rotated 45 degrees, with the corners of the dough facing the center of the butter block sides).

7. Enfold the dough: Fold the corners of the butter block up and over to the center of the dough. The butter block should completely cover the dough. Pinch the seams of the butter block together to prevent the dough from peeking through.*

Whenever folding butter, it's important to work quickly to ensure it doesn't melt. It helps if your work surface and kitchen/room are cool.

8. Make the first fold (day before): Generously flour a work surface and rolling pin. You'll need a rather large work surface for this task. With the rolling pin, using steady, even pressure, roll the butter-covered dough out from the center vertically so it triples in length and increases in width by about one and a half times, and is about ¼ inch (6 mm) thick.*

Keeping the shape of the dough is very important at this point to ensure even layers.

9. Place the dough so the longer sides run left to right. From the right side, fold one-third of the dough onto itself, keeping the edges lined up with each other. From the left side, fold one-third of the dough on top of the side that has already been folded. Line up all the edges so you're left with an even rectangle.*

In the lamination process, this is known as a "letter fold," since the dough is being folded as if it were a piece of paper going into an envelope.

10. Rest the dough: Wrap the dough in plastic wrap and refrigerate for 15 to 20 minutes to rest.*

* Resting the dough relaxes the gluten and keeps the butter chilled.

11. Make the second and third folds (day before): Remove the chilled dough from the fridge and unwrap. It should be firm, but not hard. If it's not pliable, let it sit out briefly to soften. Place on a lightly floured work surface, with the open seams at the top and bottom. With a rolling pin, using steady, even pressure, roll the dough out from the center vertically from top to bottom. The dough should once again triple in length and increase in width about one and a half times; this will take several passes.*

* When rolling out dough, it's always best to have the open seams on the top and bottom (rather than on the left and right sides) to ensure the layers remain even and don't slide when you are rolling.

12. Rotate the dough so the longer sides now run left to right. This time, from the right side, fold one-quarter of the dough onto itself. From the left side, fold one-quarter of the dough onto itself. The two ends should meet in the middle of the dough. Fold the dough in half where the ends meet.* Wrap the dough again in plastic wrap and refrigerate for 15 to 20 minutes to rest.

* This is known as a "double book fold," as the dough is folded inward and then again a second time to resemble a closed book.

13. Remove the chilled dough from the fridge and unwrap. Place on a lightly floured work surface, with the open seams at the top and bottom. Make another double book fold: Once again, roll out the dough until it triples in length and increases in width one and a half times, then rotate the dough so the longer sides now run left to right. Make the double book fold, as in step 12 above. Wrap the dough in plastic wrap and refrigerate overnight.

14. Roll out the puff pastry (day of): Remove the puff pastry from the fridge and unwrap. Place it on a lightly floured work surface. With a rolling pin, using steady, even pressure, roll the dough out from the center until it's a square that's about ¼ inch (6 mm) thick.

recipe continues

15. Chill until ready to bake: Line a baking sheet with parchment paper. Using a paring knife and an 8-inch (20 cm) round cake pan as a guide, cut the dough into a round that's about ¾ inch (2 cm) wider than the pan (the dough will shrink slightly while baking). Place the disc on the lined baking sheet, cover with plastic wrap, and chill until ready to use.

16. When ready to bake: Position a rack in the center of the oven and preheat the oven to 375°F (190°C).

17. If you're using store-bought frozen puff pastry, transfer it from the freezer into the fridge at this point to let it thaw. You want your puff pastry to be cold, but not frozen, when ready to bake.

MAKE THE CARAMELIZED APPLES

18. Make a dry caramel: Place a medium saucepan over medium heat. When the pot is hot, sprinkle a thin, even layer of sugar over the bottom of the pan. As the sugar melts and caramelizes, slowly sprinkle in the rest of the sugar, one small handful at a time, stirring gently with a silicone spatula and making sure each handful of sugar has reached a golden amber brown color before adding another handful.* Once all the sugar has been added, cook until it has turned golden amber brown, 1 to 2 minutes. Remove from the heat immediately to keep it from burning.

* You can move the pot on and off the heat to control the temperature to make sure your sugar doesn't burn and instead stays a golden amber brown.

19. Finish the caramel: Whisk the butter into the caramel, stirring until combined. Pour the caramel immediately into the bottom of an 8-inch (20 cm) round cake pan (be careful, the caramel is extremely hot).

20. Add the apples: Place the apple halves into the pan, standing up and nesting against each other, in a spiral pattern. Put as many apples as you can—you want the pan to be fully *PACKED* with apples, as they'll cook down significantly.

21. Bake the apples: Set the cake pan on a baking sheet. Lay a silicone baking mat on top of the cake pan (this prevents the tops of the apples from burning and keeps the moisture in). Bake until the apples are tender, about 1 hour.

22. Remove the silicone mat and continue to bake until the apples are soft and the caramel has thickened, 30 to 45 minutes (the liquid should have evaporated from the bottom of the pan and you'll be left with a beautifully golden caramel. Some apple varieties are juicier than others, so if you see there's still a lot of liquid, continue baking for a few more minutes).*

　*Every 15 minutes, as the apples are caramelizing in this step, use a
　metal spoon or the flat base of a small metal measuring cup to gently
　push down on the apples to flatten them into a nice even layer.*

23. Add the puff pastry: Remove the apple Tatin from the oven. Remove the chilled puff pastry disc from the fridge.* Using a fork, dock the puff pastry (gently poke holes evenly across the surface of the dough; this allows the steam to escape during baking so the crust doesn't puff up too much or too unevenly in the oven). Lay the puff pastry over the Tatin and gently tuck the overhanging edges inside the sides of the pan and all the way down to the bottom.

　*If using store-bought puff pastry, remove from the fridge and
　use a paring knife and the cake pan as a guide to trim it into
　a disc that's about ¾ inch (2 cm) wider than the pan.*

24. Bake the Tatin: Return the pan to the oven and bake the Tatin until the puff pastry is golden brown and flaky, an additional 30 to 35 minutes.

25. Chill the tarte Tatin: Remove from the oven, transfer to the refrigerator, and let chill in the pan until cooled and the caramel has set (it should no longer be a liquid), at least 1 to 2 hours. DO NOT unmold the Tatin straight from the oven when it's hot, as it will fall apart due to the moisture from the apples.

26. When ready to serve: Preheat oven to 375°F (190°C).

recipe continues

27. Warm the Tatin for a few minutes until the caramel gets a bit liquidy again. Place a plate on top, and carefully invert and unmold the Tatin onto a plate. Spoon any extra caramel over the top. Slice and serve with a dollop of crème fraîche or vanilla ice cream.

STORAGE

Best enjoyed immediately. To store, cover tightly with plastic wrap and keep in the refrigerator for 1 to 2 days. If serving from the fridge, preheat the oven to 375°F (190°C) and warm the Tatin for a few minutes.

APRICOT VANILLA PISTACHIO ETON MESS

OF ALL THE strange dishes I've tried in my life, more than one of them were from the hands of my friends Jess and Nick. Thanks to them, I have sampled "peacamole" (the controversial *New York Times* guacamole recipe made with peas). I've stared speechless at little cream-cheese-filled strawberries that looked like Santa Claus in his hat. And yes, I've even witnessed a full-fledged nacho "stadium" made of tortilla chips and dip decorated like a football field in sour cream.

In the beginning, this husband-and-wife duo were nervous. It's one thing to cook for a chef; it's another to serve a chef a dessert in the shape of a turkey made out of cereal and melted marshmallow, and stuffed with M&Ms. But as the years rolled by, my looks of shock only fueled their excitement. Soon, at every group gathering, I would be on the lookout for what Nick and Jess had brought.

They became my source of education for all things ranging from whoopie pies to bubble tea. Regardless of how busy their schedules were, they would always deliver. And sure enough, when my first cookbook came out, they got their hands on a copy and managed to bake a blue and purple cake from the recipes, which I never imagined. But that's the joy of cooking, isn't it? To jump in, get your hands dirty, and have friends who are courageous and open-minded enough to try a bite.

Nowadays, I always think of the two of them whenever there's a potluck or game night gathering. I realized that throughout the years I had never given them a recipe they could easily execute at home. The Eton mess immediately came to mind. A delightful mixture of meringue, fruit, and cream that looks like someone has dropped it on the floor. Yet somehow it's made even more delicious stirred together rather than carefully laid out, as the textures meld and the flavors blend in a beautiful mess.

INGREDIENTS

Pistachio Whipped Ganache

3 grams	1 teaspoon	unflavored gelatin powder
9 grams	1¾ teaspoons	water
66 grams	½ cup	chopped white chocolate
58 grams	¼ cup	pistachio paste
170 grams	¾ cup	heavy cream #1
25 grams	2 tablespoons	granulated sugar
170 grams	¾ cup	heavy cream #2

Vanilla Meringue

166 grams	6 large	egg whites
333 grams	2¾ cups	powdered sugar

Vanilla seeds (scraped from 1 vanilla bean) or ½ teaspoon vanilla extract

Apricot Amaretto Compote

27 grams	2 tablespoons	unsalted butter
380 grams	8 to 10	fresh apricots (pitted and halved)
35 grams	3 tablespoons	granulated sugar
14 grams	4 teaspoons	dark brown sugar
50 grams	⅓ cup	apricot nectar or juice
7 grams	1½ teaspoons	cornstarch
28 grams	5½ teaspoons	amaretto (optional)

Assembly

8 to 10 fresh apricots, pitted and sliced

Roasted pistachios

EQUIPMENT

Small bowl

Whisk

Heatproof bowl

Medium pot

Silicone spatula

Immersion blender (optional)

18 × 13-inch (46 × 33 cm) sheet pan, at least 1 inch (2.5 cm) deep

Silicone baking mat or parchment paper

Stand mixer

Digital thermometer

Rubber spatula

Large bowl

MAKE THE PISTACHIO WHIPPED GANACHE

1. Bloom the gelatin: In a small bowl, whisk together the gelatin and water until dissolved. Let the mixture sit a few minutes until the gelatin has bloomed (when it has absorbed the majority of the liquid, gaining 2 to 3 times its original volume, and feels firm and set).

2. Make the ganache: In a heatproof bowl, combine the white chocolate, pistachio paste, and the gelatin mixture.

3. In a medium pot, combine the heavy cream #1 (¾ cup/170 g) and sugar and bring to a boil while whisking. Remove from the heat and pour the hot cream mixture over the white chocolate/pistachio paste/gelatin in the bowl. Let sit for a minute or two to allow the white chocolate to melt. Stir with a silicone spatula until smooth (you can also use an immersion blender or hand blender to blend until smooth).

4. Chill the ganache: Add heavy cream #2 (¾ cup/170 g). Stir or use an immersion blender to blend until smooth. Cover with plastic wrap that touches the surface of the ganache to prevent a skin from forming. Refrigerate for a few hours, or up to overnight, until the ganache fully sets (it should no longer be a liquid). Keep chilled until ready to serve.

MAKE THE VANILLA MERINGUE

5. Preheat the oven to 175°F (80°C). Line an 18 × 13-inch (46 × 33 cm) sheet pan with a silicone baking mat or parchment paper.

recipe continues

6. Make the egg white mixture: In a stand mixer fitted with the whisk, combine the egg whites, powdered sugar, and vanilla seeds (or extract) and whip on low speed until combined.

7. Heat the meringue mixture: Fill a medium pot with about 3 inches of water and bring to a simmer over medium heat. Set the stand mixer bowl over the pot of simmering water.* Heat the egg white mixture while whisking continuously with a hand-held whisk, until it reaches 113°F (45°C) on a digital thermometer.** Remove from the heat.

 * *Make sure the bottom of the bowl does not touch the simmering water; otherwise the egg whites might scramble.*

 ** *It's important to use a thermometer when making meringues, as the egg whites need to reach a precise temperature in order to achieve the correct fluffy meringue texture.*

8. Whip the meringue: Return the mixer bowl to the stand mixer. Whip the warm egg white mixture on high speed until stiff peaks form, 5 to 7 minutes. At this point, the meringue will be light and fluffy and about tripled in volume.

9. Bake the meringue: Transfer the meringue to the lined sheet pan.* Using a rubber spatula, gently spread the meringue into one even layer all the way to the edges of the pan. Bake until the meringue has fully dried (when you peel away the silicone mat or parchment and touch the bottom of the meringue, it should no longer be wet; if there are still wet spots, keep baking until fully dried throughout). The meringue should be crisp all the way through.

 * *This is a Swiss meringue, meaning that the meringue is cooked twice—first when you heat it over simmering water, and then again when it's baked in the oven. This type of meringue has a thin, crunchy exterior, and depending on how long you bake it, the interior can either be crunchy throughout or soft and moist.*

10. Remove from the oven. Let the meringue fully cool on the sheet pan (be careful not to touch it too much, as it might deflate).

recipe continues

MAKE THE APRICOT AMARETTO COMPOTE

11. Cook the apricots: In a medium saucepan, melt the butter over medium heat. Add half of the apricots, the granulated sugar, and the brown sugar. Cover and cook over medium heat, stirring occasionally, until the apricots are tender, about 15 minutes. Stir in the remaining apricots and cook until tender, about 10 minutes longer.

12. In a small bowl, whisk together the apricot nectar and cornstarch. Pour this over the apricots. Add the amaretto (if using). Cook for a few more minutes until the mixture has thickened and the liquid has evaporated.

13. Let the compote fully chill in the fridge until ready to serve.

ASSEMBLE THE ETON MESS

14. Break the meringue into pieces: Using the back of a spoon or your hands, break the meringue into bite-size pieces.

15. Whip the pistachio ganache: Get the chilled pistachio ganache* out of the fridge and transfer it to a stand mixer fitted with the whisk. Whip on high speed until light and fluffy, a few minutes.** (You can also use a mixing bowl and hand mixer.) Use immediately.

 * *Make sure the ganache is cold when whipping. If it's at room temperature, it won't whip up into that light fluffy texture.*

 ** *As the ganache chilled in the fridge, it set and became quite thick and dense. In order to get a light and fluffy texture for this Eton Mess, the ganache is whipped so it becomes airy and spreadable.*

16. Build the Eton Mess: In a large bowl, place a generous layer of whipped pistachio ganache at the base. Top with a layer of apricot compote, followed by a layer of meringue pieces. Repeat with more ganache, compote, and meringue. Top with fresh apricot slices and finish with a sprinkle of roasted pistachios.

STORAGE

Enjoy the Eton Mess immediately! You want the meringue to maintain that crunchy texture; if stored in the refrigerator, the meringue will become soggy. Unwhipped ganache can be stored in an airtight container, with plastic wrap pressed against the surface to prevent a skin from forming, in the refrigerator for up to 3 days.

EARL GREY BRIOCHE FRENCH TOAST WITH ORANGE BLOSSOM MAPLE SYRUP

"YOU DON'T REMEMBER US," said a member of the group sitting at our outside garden table, "but we remember you."

I apologized as I didn't recognize anyone in the group of young women. They quickly explained that they used to live right down the block from the bakery and always had their Sunday breakfasts here. It was back at a time when all three friends shared a small apartment in a four-story walk-up and sought to blaze their own paths in New York City. Cold winters, high rents, and long hours at work made it hard to stay a New Yorker, and when the lease came up for their apartment, they left and each went their own way. Two to the West Coast and one to Florida. "A lot more sunlight," one of them said.

Still, something about this city—as tough and rugged as it can be—makes it so that no other place compares. So, in this rare moment when the three of them were in town, they decided to reunite. They told me that all the challenges back then now appear as precious memories.

"Can you believe it? I even miss the subway and the snowy winters," one of them giggled.

"That's where you come in, chef," said another. "The last thing we did was wait in line at your bakery. And even though we complained about how long the wait was and how cold it was that day, now that we look back at it, it was a lot of fun." They told me they had made a promise to one another that when they all reunited in New York the last thing they ate together would be their first meal back.

"That way we can get started right where we left off," one of them said.

When good friends and good food meet again, it's like no time has passed. I can't remember what it was they ate that day, but I always picture them having French toast for brunch, catching up on the time lost and yet feeling like no time has passed at all. I've never forgotten their little tradition of eating the same thing the next time they reunited, and I have since made it a little tradition of my own.

INGREDIENTS

Orange Blossom Maple Syrup

1 to 2 drops of orange blossom water

| 300 grams | 1 cup + 1 tablespoon | maple syrup |

Earl Grey Brioche French Toast

15 grams	½ ounce	Earl Grey tea leaves
245 grams	1 cup	whole milk
315 grams	1⅓ cups + 2 tablespoons	heavy cream
234 grams	5 large	eggs
204 grams	⅔ cup	maple syrup
1 gram	¼ teaspoon	salt
10 grams	2 teaspoons	rum (optional)

6 to 8 thick (1 inch/2.5 cm) slices Brioche Loaf* (page 32), day old

Unsalted butter, for cooking

Vegetable oil or canola oil, for cooking

For Serving

Powdered sugar, for dusting

Fresh fruit or your favorite toppings

I like using brioche for my French toast, as it's got a buttery, eggy, and subtly sweet flavor that works really well for this recipe. You can slice it however you'd like and it holds its shape once soaked. If you don't have brioche, this recipe also works with baguette, sourdough, or simple white bread.

EQUIPMENT

Small bowl	Baking sheet
Whisk	Wide shallow bowl
Spice or coffee grinder	Nonstick skillet
Medium pot	Spatula
Immersion blender	

MAKE THE ORANGE BLOSSOM MAPLE SYRUP

1. In a small bowl, stir the orange blossom water into the maple syrup. Whisk or stir with a spatula to combine. If you like, you can add more orange blossom water to taste.

MAKE THE EARL GREY BRIOCHE FRENCH TOAST

2. Place the tea leaves in a spice or coffee grinder. Blitz the leaves into a fine powder.

3. Infuse the milk and cream: In a medium pot, combine the milk, cream, and tea. Blend with an immersion blender. Bring to a simmer over medium heat to let the tea flavor infuse, while stirring occasionally with a whisk. Remove from the heat. Let stand for 10 to 20 minutes to cool slightly.

4. Make the custard: Whisk in the eggs, maple syrup, salt, and rum (if using) until smooth. Make sure to mix thoroughly, so you don't end up with bits of egg yolk or white as the French toast sears in the pan.*

 To ensure a smooth and even mixture, use an immersion blender.

5. Preheat the oven to 350°F.

6. Toast the brioche: Arrange the slices on a baking sheet and toast until just golden blond, 3 to 5 minutes. Remove from the oven and let cool for a few minutes. (Toasting the brioche first allows more of the custard soak to absorb.)

7. Soak the bread: Transfer the custard mixture to a wide shallow bowl. Soak the toasted brioche in the custard, fully submerging the slices and turning them over after a few minutes so they soak generously and evenly. Give the slices a little squeeze to make sure they've absorbed a good amount of the mixture.

8. Transfer the soaked slices to a baking sheet and let them rest for 1 to 2 minutes. (Press the slices with your fingers—they should feel damp but not so wet that they lose their structure and shape.)

recipe continues

9. Cook the French toast: In a nonstick skillet, heat 2 tablespoons butter and 2 tablespoons oil over medium heat. Get the pan good and hot.* Sear the soaked bread slices for a few minutes until golden brown and caramelized on one side. Flip and continue on the other side, for another few minutes. Add more butter and oil to the pan as necessary and continue with the remaining slices. (You can keep them warm in the oven or loosely covered with foil while you're cooking the remaining slices, until ready to serve.)

 * *Make sure that your pan is hot before you add the bread slices. If the pan isn't hot enough, the liquid will leak out from the bread, rather than searing and caramelizing.*

10. Serve with orange blossom maple syrup, a dusting of powdered sugar, and fresh fruits or your favorite toppings.

STORAGE

Best enjoyed right away.

THE ULTIMATE COOKIE: BROWN BUTTER, DARK CHOCOLATE, WALNUT & SEA SALT COOKIES

I MUST ADMIT, I was nervous about judging a cookie competition for the holiday season. First, because French chefs aren't necessarily known to be experts in cookies, a real American institution. But also because I wasn't sure how many cookies I could physically eat in one sitting. Yet there I was, a head judge for this annual cookie competition. The contest started promptly at noon, and I arrived twenty minutes early to start preparing.

To my surprise, there were less than a handful of entrants on the table. A decorated box of sugar cookies with intricate piping sat next to a thumbprint cookie. There was a pretty plate of raspberry Linzer cookies delicately covered in powdered sugar. Maybe just four entrants in total. A volunteer was numbering the cookies and laying them out.

I sat down at the judges' table and was ready to begin. A group of people in the distance slowly approached. "I hope those spectators won't be too disappointed by the lack of entrants this year," I said. As they drew closer, just two minutes before the clock struck noon, I realized that they were all holding small Tupperware boxes. They were also entrants in the contest. How strange, I thought. Why would everyone be so last-minute with entering their cookies?

Then I took my first bite. A few cookies in, it dawned on me. Every single one of the later entrants were all freshly baked cookies that were still warm!

The seasoned competitors knew that even the best recipe couldn't trump the allure of cookies still warm from the oven. Ultimately, a victor was chosen. It was a walnut, sea salt, chocolate chip cookie. Crispy edges, soft chewy center, with just the right amount of crunch from the nuts. The winner of the competition understandably didn't disclose his recipe to me. But the little tip on freshly baked was priceless in

itself: I also like to preshape the dough and keep it frozen so I can bake cookies to order.

Inspired by the winner's flavors, walnuts and sea salt became a favorite combination. And for extra nuttiness, I like to simmer my butter until browned prior to adding it to the batter. The key, of course, is baking the cookies fresh and serving them right out of the oven.

MAKES 10 TO 12 LARGE COOKIES

INGREDIENTS

100 grams	7 tablespoons (3½ oz)	unsalted butter #1, cubed
120 grams	1½ cups	walnuts
150 grams	1 stick + 3 tablespoons (5½ oz)	unsalted butter #2, at room temperature and cubed
120 grams	½ cup + 1 tablespoon	granulated sugar
120 grams	½ cup packed + 1½ tablespoons	light brown sugar
75 grams	2 large	eggs
330 grams	2½ cups	all-purpose flour
4 grams	1½ teaspoons	salt
2 grams	½ teaspoon	baking soda
120 grams	¾ cup	dark chocolate chunks/chips

Maldon sea salt, for finishing

Dark chocolate chunks/chips, for finishing (optional)

EQUIPMENT

Small pot	Baking sheet
Silicone spatula	Parchment paper
Various bowls	Whisk

1. Make the brown butter: In a small pot,* melt butter #1 (7 tablespoons/100 g) over medium heat, stirring occasionally with a silicone spatula and swirling around the pan to help the butter melt evenly. After 3 to 5 minutes, the butter

recipe continues

will start to foam. Continue cooking for a few more minutes, until it turns light golden brown and there's a nutty, lightly toasted aroma. Remove from the heat and transfer to a bowl (so the butter doesn't continue to cook or burn).

* Using a light-colored pot helps when browning butter, so you can easily watch the coloring. It's harder to tell in a darker pan, and the butter may overbrown and burn.

2. Preheat the oven to 350°F (175°C). Line a baking sheet with parchment paper.

3. Toast the nuts: Arrange the walnuts on the baking sheet and bake until lightly toasted, 9 to 11 minutes. When cool enough to handle, roughly chop and set aside.

4. Combine the wet ingredients: In a large bowl, combine the cubed butter #2 (11 tablespoons/150 g), granulated sugar, and brown sugar. Scrape in the warm brown butter. Mix with a whisk until combined and the mixture becomes lighter in texture, a few minutes. Add the eggs and mix until incorporated.

5. Combine the dry ingredients: In a bowl, whisk together the flour, salt, and baking soda.

6. Make the dough: Slowly add the dry ingredients to the wet ingredients in three additions, making sure the dry ingredients are incorporated before each one. Mix until just combined. Fold in the chocolate chunks or chips and the chopped walnuts with a rubber spatula until evenly distributed.

7. Bake the cookies: Roll the dough into balls about 2 inches (5 cm) in diameter, about 100 grams each, and place on the baking sheet. Press down gently to slightly flatten them into discs. Sprinkle a few flecks of Maldon sea salt on each cookie (you can add a few extra chocolate chunks on top, too). Bake until the edges are golden and the center is still soft, 9 to 11 minutes. Let cool until warm, then enjoy.

STORAGE

Best enjoyed immediately. To store, place in an airtight container and keep at room temperature for 1 to 2 days.

ORANGE YUZU MARMALADE

I NEVER THOUGHT of jam in the same category as wine, but a welcome gift from a friend of mine in Hong Kong made me see it in a new light. Susan's "love language" was food. Whether she was saying "hello," "good-bye," or "thank you," there was always something edible exchanged. Since my first visits to Hong Kong over a decade ago, my luggage has always been filled with bottles of jams and sauces from Susan to bring back home. And I started noticing over the years that she labeled the jars with not only the name of the fruit but also the year.

I loved that her jams came in "vintages." And like with a bottle of Bordeaux, every year the harvests and fruits would yield different results. She used rare fruits that I wasn't able to source in the US that reflected the terroir of the region. From Alphonso mangoes from India to sour cherries she hand-carried from Istanbul—each little jar was a time capsule.

When I think about the perfect souvenir and gift for out-of-town guests, I always am inspired by Susan. This orange marmalade is a citrus recipe that I have always loved. And I picture someone waking up at home on a weekend morning being able to taste something fresh and bright kept pristine and preserved from across the world and in a different time.

MAKES 3 TO 4 CUPS

INGREDIENTS

182 grams	2½ cups	finely chopped orange zest* (from 10 to 12 oranges)
230 grams	1 cup	orange juice
230 grams	1 cup	yuzu juice
180 grams	¾ cup + 1 tablespoon	sugar

* Use a vegetable peeler to take off just the zest (the thin orange-colored layer) in thin strips and not any of the spongy white pith underneath.

recipe continues

EQUIPMENT

Medium pot

Fine-mesh sieve

Silicone spatula or wooden spoon

1. **Blanch the orange zest:** In a medium pot, combine the orange zest and enough water to fully submerge the zest and simmer over medium heat for 5 minutes (the liquid will start to cook down and evaporate). Stir occasionally with a silicone spatula or wooden spoon. Drain in a fine-mesh sieve, reserving just the zest.

2. Return the zest to the pot, add more water, again enough to fully submerge the zest. Simmer again for 5 more minutes until the liquid cooks down. Drain. Repeat this process once more (this helps to remove the bitterness from the zest). Drain.

3. **Cook the marmalade:** Return the zest to the pot and add the orange juice, yuzu juice, and sugar. Simmer over medium heat to cook slowly while stirring occasionally, until the liquid is cooked down and the mixture becomes thick and jammy, 15 to 20 minutes.

4. Let fully cool. Enjoy scooped over a bowl of ice cream, on your morning toast or pancakes, or mixed into yogurt.

STORAGE

To store, transfer the marmalade to a jar or other airtight container and keep in the refrigerator for 1 to 2 weeks. If you want to preserve your marmalade for longer, you may need to purchase jam jars with accompanying lids. Boil the lids and the jars to sterilize, dry thoroughly, and fill with the jam to the top. Turn the jars upside down in water, fully submerged, and boil for 10 to 15 minutes. Once cooled, the lids will seal tightly and the jam will last for several months if unopened.

CINNAMON ROLLS
WITH MAPLE MASCARPONE ICING

"THE KIDS ARE out of the house!" said one of our managers with both fear and relief. Her daughters had both graduated, moved out post college, and were now "adulting" daily in their very first apartment together. They built their IKEA tables and painted the walls themselves. And now it was time for them to officially start cooking.

Curiously, the girls insisted that the first thing they bake in the apartment be a round shape. "I heard it's good luck to bake something round," one of them said as they started digging into my repertoire of recipes. The first few items were rejected. Cookies were the right shape, but too simple and not celebratory enough. Donuts were too much hassle. They didn't have a Bundt pan to bake with and needed something free-form. So finally, we settled on the cinnamon roll.

The girls got right to it. After stocking their pantry with their first spice rack, they used the cinnamon for their schmear. Together, they mixed the dough, let it proof, punched it down, and eventually rolled it together. As the cinnamon rolls baked, the smell filled their house and the hallways of the apartment building. It was how they first met some of their neighbors, who came out when the smell of the cinnamon rolls beckoned.

The girls lived together for four years before moving out and getting their own places. To this day they swear that the round cinnamon rolls gave them luck in settling in and meeting new neighbors, and baking them is a tradition they do in every new place they've lived in since.

MAKES 8 LARGE CINNAMON ROLLS

INGREDIENTS

Brioche Dough

2 kilograms	double recipe	Brioche Dough (page 34)

Cinnamon Schmear

540 grams	2⅔ cups packed	dark brown sugar
360 grams	3 sticks (12 oz)	unsalted butter, melted
34 grams	4½ tablespoons	ground cinnamon
70 grams	2 large	egg whites

Egg Wash

100 grams	2 large	eggs
10 grams	2 teaspoons	whole milk
2 grams	½ teaspoon	salt

Maple Mascarpone Icing

400 grams	2 cups + 2 tablespoons	mascarpone
400 grams	1½ cups + 2½ tablespoons	maple syrup

EQUIPMENT

Large bowl	Offset spatula
Whisk	9 × 13-inch (23 × 33 cm) baking dish
Baking sheet	Small Bowl
Parchment Paper	Pastry brush
Rolling pin	

MAKE THE BRIOCHE DOUGH (DAY BEFORE)

1. Make the brioche dough as directed through the second fermentation (step 7) and refrigerate overnight.

MAKE THE CINNAMON SCHMEAR (DAY BEFORE OR DAY OF)

2. In a large bowl, stir together the brown sugar, melted butter, and cinnamon. Add the egg whites and whisk until thoroughly combined.

3. Shape and proof the cinnamon roll: Line a baking sheet with parchment paper. Lightly flour a flat work surface. Using a rolling pin, roll out the dough into a rectangle that is about ⅛ inch (3 mm) thick and roughly 19½ × 25½ inches (50 × 65 cm). Set the rectangle with a long side facing you. With an offset spatula, generously spread the cinnamon schmear over the top of the dough in one even layer, leaving a ¾-inch (2 cm) border along the top edge. Starting at the bottom edge, carefully roll the dough up tightly with your fingertips so it forms a long horizontal log. Transfer the log to the lined baking sheet and refrigerate for at least 30 to 45 minutes.

4. Cut the spirals: Remove the chilled dough from the refrigerator and cut slices roughly 1½ inches (4 cm) thick. Place the rolls cut side up in a deep 9 × 13-inch (23 × 233 cm) baking dish. You'll be able to fit 8 cinnamon rolls in the dish, 2 rows of 4 rolls across.

5. Proof the rolls: Cover the baking dish loosely with plastic wrap and let the dough proof in a warm area slightly above room temperature until they've doubled in size, 1½ to 2½ hours (the rolls should be touching at this point).

6. Preheat oven: Position a rack in the center of the oven and preheat the oven to 350°F (175°C).

MAKE THE EGG WASH

7. In a small bowl, whisk together the eggs, milk, and salt.

8. Bake the cinnamon rolls: With a pastry brush, lightly egg wash the tops of the cinnamon rolls. Bake until golden brown on top, 30 to 35 minutes, rotating the pan front to back halfway through (to check for doneness, the center of the rolls should spring back when pressed gently).

recipe continues

9. Let cool for 10 to 15 minutes before frosting (if you frost when the cinnamon rolls are just out of the oven and too hot, the frosting will melt). While cooling, make the frosting.

MAKE THE MAPLE MASCARPONE ICING

10. In a bowl, whisk together the mascarpone and maple syrup until smooth.

11. Glaze the cinnamon rolls: Using an offset or rubber spatula, generously spread the maple mascarpone icing on top of the warm cinnamon rolls. Serve immediately.

STORAGE

Best enjoyed when the cinnamon rolls are still warm.

FAREWELL

CHOCOLATE PEANUT BUTTER CANDY BAR

"FAREWELLS TASTE LIKE a chocolate candy bar," said Paul. The first time I heard that statement, I was confused. But Paul had probably experienced farewells much more than I had.

Paul's father was a diplomat. And that meant he was stationed in different cities around the world for short stints averaging two to four years at a time. From France to Vietnam to New York to Dubai. Between kindergarten and senior year in high school, Paul had been to eight different schools, each in a different country. I met him in the brief two years when he was in New York.

For Paul, the last few days before yet another big move are always a blur. They're filled with packing, cleaning, and inevitably forgetting things. "The one calm moment," he said, "is when you finally get on that plane and take off. As you sit there in silence with nothing but the humming of the engines as you see the city below you miniaturize—that's when you actually realize you're saying good-bye."

Since Paul wasn't a fan of airplane food, he always stocked up on snacks in the shops in the terminal. His go-to was a chocolate candy bar, which he would unwrap and eat once he boarded the plane. Up in the air, between where he had been and where he was going, this chocolate bar would be his last meal.

So I decided to create a recipe inspired by Paul—a candy bar dipped in dark chocolate for rich bitter contrast to the crunchy and nutty interior. *Feuilletine*, or small shards of thin crêpe-like wafers, add a crispiness to each bite. Paul's final meal wasn't a generous dinner among friends or a visit to his favorite eatery. But fittingly, like all good-byes, it was bittersweet.

MAKES 12 CANDY BARS

INGREDIENTS

Peanut Butter Feuilletine

27 grams	2 tablespoons	unsalted butter, at room temperature
100 grams	¾ cup	milk chocolate chips or chopped chunks
238 grams	1 cup + 1 tablespoon	peanut butter
135 grams	1⅔ cups	feuilletine

Milk Chocolate Ganache

362 grams	3 cups	milk chocolate chips or chopped chunks
11 grams	1 tablespoon	cacao paste
65 grams	4½ tablespoons	unsalted butter, at room temperature
225 grams	1 cup	heavy cream
80 grams	½ cup	roughly chopped peanuts
2 grams	1 teaspoon	Maldon sea salt

15 to 20 peanuts, for topping

Dark Chocolate Dip

300 grams	2 cups	dark chocolate chips or chopped chunks
120 grams	1 cup	cocoa butter

Maldon salt, for sprinkling

EQUIPMENT

Medium pot	8-inch (20 cm) square baking dish
Heatproof bowl	Fork or toothpicks
Silicone and rubber spatulas	Wire rack
Parchment paper	

recipe continues

MAKE THE PEANUT BUTTER FEUILLETINE

1. Melt the chocolate mixture: Fill a pot with 2 to 3 inches of water and bring to a simmer over medium heat. In a heatproof bowl (that will fit snugly over the pot*), combine the butter, milk chocolate, and peanut butter. Set the bowl over the pot (there should be a few inches of space between the bottom of the bowl and the top of the water). Gently stir everything together with a silicone spatula until it becomes smooth and melted. Remove the bowl from the heat.

This is called a double boiler, which is used to gently melt chocolate using the heat/steam coming off the water.

2. Add the feuilletine to the melted chocolate mixture and gently fold with a rubber spatula until it's evenly coated.

3. Chill the mixture: Cut a piece of parchment paper that's 8 × 12 inches (20 × 30 cm). Line an 8-inch (20 cm) square baking dish with the parchment (the overhanging ends of parchment are so you can easily lift the candy bars out of the baking dish later). Pour in the chocolate mixture and spread it in one even layer using a spatula. Refrigerate until firm.

MEANWHILE, MAKE THE MILK CHOCOLATE GANACHE

4. In a heatproof bowl, combine the milk chocolate, cacao paste, and butter.

5. In a medium pot, heat the cream over medium heat, stirring occasionally. Once it starts to simmer, remove from the heat (do not boil).

6. Pour the hot cream over the chocolate mixture. Let it sit for 3 to 5 minutes until the chocolate starts to melt. Mix with a spatula until smooth. Let cool at room temperature for 10 minutes.

7. Sprinkle in the chopped peanuts and sea salt and fold with a spatula to combine.

8. Layer the ganache over the feuilletine: Remove the peanut butter feuilletine from the fridge (it should be chilled and hardened at this point). Pour the chocolate ganache over the feuilletine, spreading with a spatula until smooth and level.

9. Freeze the candy: Cover with plastic wrap and freeze until the ganache is solid, a few hours, or up to overnight.

10. Cut into bars: Remove the baking dish from the freezer. Use the sides of the parchment to lift the whole chocolate peanut butter square out of the dish and place it on a cutting board or baking sheet (still on the parchment). Use a sharp knife to cut into bars that are 3½ × ¾ inch (9 cm × 2 cm).

11. Top and freeze: Top with peanuts (press them into the ganache so they stick) and return the bars to the freezer to chill while you make the dark chocolate dip.

MAKE THE DARK CHOCOLATE DIP

12. In a medium pot, bring 2 to 3 inches of water to a simmer. In a heatproof bowl (that will fit snugly over the pot), combine the dark chocolate and cocoa butter and set over the pot, stirring with a silicone spatula until melted and smooth.

13. Dip the bars: Remove the bars from the freezer. Using a fork or toothpicks, dip the individual bars (still frozen) into the warm chocolate dip. Shake off any excess chocolate and place the bars on a wire rack or parchment paper and allow the chocolate to set.

14. Finish the bars with a sprinkle of sea salt and enjoy.

STORAGE

To store, place in an airtight container and keep in the refrigerator for up to 3 days.

CHAPTER 3
Love

Johnny Cash once sang: "The taste of love is sweet." And from my experience, it's true. From first dates to going down on one knee and popping the question, pastries have always been a celebration of love in our lives.

FIRST DATES

BELGIAN LIÈGE WAFFLES

A JOURNALIST ONCE approached me with a theory that our bakery was the perfect location for a first date. She methodically broke it down for me:

- It's less of a commitment than a full meal or dinner. If the chemistry isn't there, it's a quick in and out.
- It's affordable and casual.
- It's suitable for all ages.
- If there's a line (which there often is), it can be an indicator of your date's patience level and a chance to catch up on the conversation.

"And lastly, morning people and dessert people—well, those are my kind of people," she said.

I chuckled. It was something I had never thought about until that moment.

But ever since then, I noticed first dates in our bakery everywhere I looked. Filled with curiosity and eagerness, they are easy to spot. Sometimes one person scopes out the space a few minutes before his or her date arrives. If it's someone who's a fan, they would've called in to preorder their items. Other times, the most telling sign is a giggling handshake or a polite hug. A joke to break the ice; courteous questions asked with a smile. I wondered how so many of those dates worked out, but never knew the ending once they walked out the door.

In many ways, there are lots of "first date" moments in baking. Every time you test out a new recipe, you are taking a leap of faith. You're learning something. You are trying to follow the right steps, but things can go wrong. And ultimately, you're trying to find out if there's true love on the other end in the form of something that matches your tastes exactly.

A few years back a guest with his newborn baby and his wife stopped me while they were waiting in line. He let me know that they had waited in line on their first date and come back every year on their anniversary to relive it. He said that he had, funnily enough, prepared a prebreakfast for his now wife in case she got hungry in line.

"I made some waffles that I was keeping warm in a bag because it was a cold winter day," he told me. "I thought he was a total dork," she laughed.

And now they are a trio. It gave me a sense of comfort to think that maybe the journalist's theory was right all along, and the bakery was in some way a secret ingredient to a successful first date. In his honor, this Liège waffle recipe goes out to our morning people, to our dessert lovers, and to those hopeful first daters.

MAKES 8 TO 10 WAFFLES OR 18 TO 20 MINI WAFFLES

INGREDIENTS

7 grams	2½ teaspoons	active dry yeast
92 grams	⅓ cup	water, at room temperature
18 grams	1½ tablespoons	light brown sugar
315 grams	2 cups + 2 tablespoons	all-purpose flour
1 gram	¼ teaspoon	salt
169 grams	4 large	eggs
225 grams	2 sticks (8 oz)	unsalted butter, melted
169 grams	1 cup	pearl sugar
Cooking spray		

EQUIPMENT

Small bowl	Stand mixer with a dough hook
Whisk	Waffle maker

1. Make the dough: In a small bowl, whisk together the yeast and water until dissolved.

2. In a stand mixer fitted with the dough hook, mix the brown sugar, flour, and salt on medium speed until combined.

3. Continuing on medium speed, add the eggs one at a time, mixing well after each addition. Add the yeast mixture and mix until combined. Gradually stream in the melted butter and mix until evenly combined.

4. Let the dough rise: Cover the bowl with plastic wrap and let the dough rest for approximately 30 minutes (it will rise to about double in size, but still look loose).*

  Once the dough has risen, you can use it immediately, or you can make it ahead of time and keep in the fridge overnight until ready to use.

5. Using your hands, scoop up balls of dough the size of golf balls. Flatten gently into a disc with your hands and dip one side in the pearl sugar. Fold the edges of the dough over to fully cover the pearl sugar inside each waffle.

6. Preheat a waffle maker until hot and mist with cooking spray. Drop a ball of dough into each waffle mold. Cook the waffles according to the manufacturer's directions until light golden brown.

7. Serve immediately while warm, or wrap some up to go with a thermos of coffee for your breakfast date. *Bonne chance!*

STORAGE

Best enjoyed immediately. To store, cover with plastic wrap or place in an airtight container and keep at room temperature for 1 to 2 days (they can be enjoyed at room temp or warmed in the oven for a few minutes).

SOURDOUGH LOAF

"A SPECIAL REQUEST from the guest," said my manager hesitantly. Out of all the off-menu items our guests have asked for, this was one of the most unexpected. Rather than a special cake or a favorite pastry, the guest wanted a little bit of levain.

In our kitchens, we talk a lot about levain, a wet doughy starter that we use as a leavener. Made from apples, water, and flour, it is left to ferment and grow, and becomes the key ingredient that helps our bread and *viennoiserie* not only to rise but also to develop a distinctive flavor. Every day, we "feed" it by adding flour to keep it alive. We've affectionally called it "the baby," and even on Christmas and New Year's Day—the only two days of the year we're closed—we discuss who will come in to "feed the baby." These days our levain is over twelve years old, and like a rolling stock, has built layer upon layer of flavor through time.

But this was the first time someone had asked to buy it. The guest explained he was a firefighter who had a passion for baking. While he battled fires in his day job, over the weekends at home, he lit them up in his oven and made sourdough.

"Weekend baking projects—it's the best way to relax," he told me, describing it as a combination of aromatherapy (that smell of fresh bread), meditation (waiting for the bread to bake), and reward (your first bite). But in order to step up his game, he wanted our levain.

We were hesitant, but eventually we packaged up some of the levain for him and sent him on his way with our blessings for his Sunday sourdough.

Sourdough can be quite an undertaking. It's all about the levain—which cannot be substituted and must be made from scratch. But don't be intimidated about rolling up your sleeves and getting your hands dirty. Bread making is about kneading the dough, punching it down, rolling it tightly. Tell yourself you will try this recipe again and again until you start to get the right feel for the dough.

A few months after the firefighter's visit, a loaf of sourdough from him sat on my desk. I remember bringing it up to our kitchen and showing it to our chefs. And we all surrounded it as if we were looking at a grandchild, a new generation of sourdough from our "mother starter."

"I can taste the family resemblance," joked one of our chefs.

MAKES 1 LOAF (SERVES 6 TO 8)

INGREDIENTS

Levain*

200 grams	1½ cups + 1½ tablespoons	all-purpose flour, plus more for feeding
200 grams	¾ cup + 5 teaspoons	water, at room temperature, plus more for feeding

Dough

348 grams	2¾ cups	bread flour #1
282 grams	1¼ cups minus 2½ teaspoons	warm water (90° to 95°F/ 32° to 35°C)
272 grams		levain (from above)
87 grams	¾ cup	bread flour #2
11 grams	2 teaspoons	salt

All-purpose flour, for dusting

* Making your own levain generally takes about 5 days, as the flour and water take time to ferment and you'll need to "feed" the mixture daily by adding flour and water to allow it to grow. This ultimately will give the bread its flavor and make the dough rise as well.

EQUIPMENT

Large glass or ceramic bowl	Stand mixer with a dough hook
Whisk	Bread proofing basket
Rubber spatula	Sharp razor blade or X-Acto blade
Large bowl	2 sheet pans

MAKE THE LEVAIN (5 DAYS BEFORE BAKING)

1. Day 1: In a large glass or ceramic mixing bowl that's at least two to three times the size of your mixture, combine 50 grams (6½ tablespoons) flour and 50 grams (3 tablespoons + 1 teaspoon) water, mixing with a whisk until evenly combined. Cover the bowl loosely with a clean kitchen towel or a cheesecloth and leave it at room temperature for 24 hours.

WHAT IS LEVAIN?

Levain, or a levain starter, is a leavening agent that's made with equal parts flour and water and is used to bake bread and *viennoiserie*. Think of it as a much more dynamic substitute for yeast. The flour and water mixture naturally ferments and as it ferments, it also grows and must be "fed" with more flour and water to keep it alive. (Many sourdough starters are a type of levain. They're what give sourdough that sourness and depth of flavor, and what give a well-made croissant that slightly yeasty fermented taste.) Here at the bakery, our levain was started in 2011 when we first opened on Spring Street, and every day since then our team has refreshed it to keep it alive. We have different levains with varying hydration levels for different pastries. Today, a piece of that original levain still lives on in each of our croissants here in our NYC bakery, and we've even brought it to our shops around the world so that there's a little piece of home there, too!

2. **Day 2:** Add another 50 grams (6½ tablespoons) flour and 50 grams (3 tablespoons + 1 teaspoon) water, mixing with a spatula until combined. Cover loosely and leave it at room temperature for another 24 hours.

3. **Day 3:** Add the remaining 100 grams (¾ cup + 2½ teaspoons) flour and 100 grams (6 tablespoons + 2 teaspoons) water, mixing with a spatula until combined. Cover loosely and leave it at room temperature for another 24 hours.

4. **Day 4:** Remove 20 percent of the levain mixture from the bowl and discard. Cover loosely and leave it at room temperature for another 24 hours.

5. **Day 5:** Now it's time to check if the levain is ready to use! It should be light and fluffy, bubbly, and have a pronounced fermented aroma without any acidity. You will be able to smell some sourness and see microbubbles.

6. **Give it a shake:** It should easily wobble and jiggle. If it's not quite there, weigh the levain and "feed" the levain with equal parts flour and water that combined are equal to the weight of the levain, until it's ready. For instance, if you have a

recipe continues

levain that is 1 kilogram, you would "feed" it with 500 grams water and 500 grams flour. (You can store the levain in an airtight container in the fridge for up to a few days.)

MAKE THE DOUGH (DAY BEFORE BAKING)

7. In a large bowl, whisk together the bread flour #1 (2¾ cups/348 g) with the warm water until evenly combined. Cover the bowl with plastic wrap and let rest for 20 to 30 minutes at room temperature.

8. Unwrap the bowl and add the levain and bread flour #2 (¾ cup/87 g). Mix by hand until well combined. Let the mixture rest in the bowl for about 10 minutes. Transfer the mixture to a stand mixer fitted with the dough hook and mix on medium speed until a dough has formed, it becomes stretchy and elastic,* and it pulls away from the sides of the bowl.

 * *To test if the dough has enough elasticity (i.e., if the gluten has developed enough), perform the Windowpane Test: Take a small piece of dough and gently stretch it between your fingers. If the dough can be stretched thin without tearing and you can see light shining through, then the gluten has developed enough and the dough is ready.*

9. Let the dough rest: Continuing to mix on medium speed, add the salt and mix until combined. Turn off the mixer, cover the bowl with a clean kitchen towel or cheesecloth, and allow the dough to rest in the bowl for about 30 minutes in a warm area slightly above room temperature.

10. Preshape the dough and rest: Transfer the dough to a well-floured work surface, sprinkle a bit of flour on top of it, and shape it into a loose round ball. Cover loosely with the kitchen towel/cheesecloth and let rest in a warm area slightly above room temperature, until the dough has doubled in size, 2 to 3 hours (the dough will still feel light and loose).

11. Prepare a bread proofing basket: Line the basket with a clean kitchen towel, then dust it heavily with flour, using your hands to rub the flour into the bottom of the cloth and up the sides. You'll end up using more flour than you think to create a layer of flour that coats the surface of the towel.

12. Stretch and fold the dough four times: Bring the top edge toward you so it meets in the middle of the dough, then bring the bottom edge up (like you're folding a piece of paper in thirds to go into an envelope). Repeat, but this time, pull the right side inward toward the center of the dough, then bring the left side inward toward the center. Reshape it into a loaf (the shape of your proofing basket will dictate the shape of your loaf: If your basket is round, make a round loaf. If oval, make an oval loaf).

13. Retard the dough: Place the ball of dough into the prepared basket with the seal on the bottom. Chill in the fridge overnight to allow the dough to rest and relax.

14. Bake the bread (day of): Position a rack in the center and one in the bottom third of the oven and preheat the oven to 450°F (230°C). Line a baking sheet with parchment paper.

15. Remove the basket from the fridge and transfer the dough to the lined baking sheet, seam side down. Using a sharp blade, such as a razor blade or an X-Acto blade, score (make shallow cuts) the top of the dough into your desired design.*

* Scoring creates "vents" to help the fermentation gases release during baking and guides the way the dough rises as it bakes, allowing the loaf to maintain its shape. If you do not score the dough, the surface may rise unevenly and you'll get a misshapen loaf.

16. Place a handful of ice cubes* onto a sheet pan and place on the lower oven rack. Bake the bread on the center rack for 15 minutes. After 15 minutes, reduce the oven temperature to 375°F (190°C) and bake until the loaf has a golden brown crust, 40 to 50 minutes more.

* The ice cubes will create steam and moisture in the oven, which help maintain moisture in the bread and gives your loaf that beautifully crisp crust.

17. Remove from the oven and let cool on a wire rack for 20 to 30 minutes. Slice and enjoy with butter and a sprinkle of sea salt.

recipe continues

STORAGE

Best enjoyed right away. To store, cover with plastic wrap and keep at room temperature for up to 1 day. You can also freeze the loaf, wrapped in plastic, for up to 2 weeks (to serve from the freezer, preheat the oven to 350°F/80°C and bake until thawed in the middle and the edges are once again crisp).

TIRAMISU

WHEN I WAS a young cook, a chef from the French embassy once told me that you should never reveal to other people what your favorite dish to eat is. The story goes that former French president Jacques Chirac made the mistake of telling everyone his preferred meal was *tête de veau*, the classic calves' head terrine (which is much more delicious than it sounds). Once word got out, every time a chef wanted to impress him, they would serve him *tête de veau*. That little bit of trivia followed the president for the rest of his life, and countless numbers of *tête de veau* later, his favorite dish had turned into one he dreaded. Too much of a favorite thing can backfire, but in my case, it is quite the opposite. I would happily eat my favorite dessert daily, *and* I declare it proudly.

It took me a while to realize what my favorite dessert is. Being a pastry chef, I am constantly trying desserts and pastries, and sometimes I have so much palate fatigue I skip dessert altogether. But as I've matured, I've became more conscious of my tastes. I'm not a fan of meringues—something about the texture reminds me of nails on a chalkboard. Most citrus desserts taste far too tart for my palate. And then one day I realized that tiramisu was the one item I always returned to on a menu. There's something about the soft mascarpone and the bitterness of the espresso that balances perfectly.

In my recipe, I teach you to make your own ladyfingers, which gives you flexibility on the shape and size as well as just a bit more tenderness in the dough after it soaks. Top generously with a velvety layer of cocoa powder. And while I hope no one will overdo it and serve me tiramisu at every meal, I also hope I can convince you to make it your favorite one day, too.

INGREDIENTS

Biscuit Cuillère (Ladyfinger Sponge)

190 grams	10 large	egg yolks
119 grams	½ cup + 1 tablespoon	sugar #1
333 grams	11 large	egg whites
119 grams	½ cup + 1 tablespoon	sugar #2
119 grams	⅔ cup + ¼ cup	cornstarch
119 grams	¾ cup + 1 tablespoon	all-purpose flour

Mascarpone Cream

400 grams	2 cups + 2 tablespoons	mascarpone
200 grams	2 cups	sugar
150 grams	⅔ cup	water
240 grams	12 large	egg yolks
400 grams	2 cups	heavy cream

Vanilla seeds (scraped from 1 vanilla bean) or ½ teaspoon vanilla extract

Coffee Syrup

600 grams	2½ cups	hot brewed coffee
115 grams	½ cup + 2 teaspoons	sugar
5 grams	2½ teaspoons	grated orange zest (from ½ orange)
50 grams	10 teaspoons	amaretto (optional)

Assembly

Cocoa powder, for finishing

recipe continues

EQUIPMENT

18 × 13-inch (46 × 33 cm) sheet pan, at least 1 inch (2.5 cm) deep

Silicone baking mat or parchment

Stand mixer (or hand mixer)

Mixing bowls

Rubber spatula

Medium pot

Digital thermometer

9 × 13-inch (23 × 33 cm) glass or ceramic baking dish at least 2½ inches (6.5 cm) deep

Pastry brush

Sifter or small fine-mesh sieve

MAKE THE BISCUIT CUILLÈRE (LADYFINGER SPONGE)

1. Preheat the oven to 410°F (210°C). Line an 18 × 13-inch (46 × 33 cm) sheet pan with a silicone baking mat or parchment paper.

2. Whip the egg yolks: In a stand mixer fitted with the whisk (or in a large bowl with a hand mixer), whip the egg yolks and sugar #1 on high speed until pale and fluffy, 2 to 3 minutes. Transfer the mixture to a bowl. Wash and fully dry the stand mixer bowl and whisk.

3. Whip the egg whites: Add the egg whites to the cleaned and dried stand mixer bowl and whip on high speed until foamy, 1 to 2 minutes. Gradually stream in sugar #2 while continuing to mix on high speed, until stiff peaks form.

4. Fold the egg whites into the yolks: Fold the egg white mixture into the yolk mixture little by little with a rubber spatula. Be very gentle and do not overmix, as you don't want the fluffy egg whites to deflate.

5. Make the batter: In a separate bowl, whisk together the cornstarch and flour until combined. Gradually add the flour mixture little by little to the egg mixture, folding gently with a rubber spatula until fully incorporated.

6. Pour the batter into the lined sheet pan until it's about three-quarters of the way full, spreading it into one even layer with a spatula.*

 * *For this recipe, instead of piping individual ladyfingers, we bake one large sheet of cake so you can cut it into rectangles once baked and assemble the tiramisu one full layer at a time.*

7. Bake the cake: Bake until the cake is lightly golden on top, 12 to 15 minutes, rotating the pan front to back halfway through baking.

8. Cool the cake: Remove from the oven and let fully cool on the baking sheet. Once cool, carefully unmold and flip the cake over and gently peel away the silicone mat or parchment. Set the cake aside until ready to assemble the tiramisu.

MAKE THE MASCARPONE CREAM

9. In a large bowl, mix the mascarpone with a rubber spatula until it's soft and spreadable.

10. Make a sugar syrup: In a medium pot, combine the sugar and water and cook over medium heat while stirring until it reaches 250°F (121°C) on a digital thermometer.

11. Meanwhile, beat the egg yolks: In a stand mixer fitted with the whisk (or in a large bowl with a hand mixer), whip the yolks on high speed until light and fluffy.

12. As soon as the sugar syrup reaches temp, remove from the heat and slowly stream it into the egg yolk mixture directly down the side of the bowl while continuing to mix on high speed, until the mixture becomes light and fluffy.

13. Fold the mascarpone into the egg mixture with a rubber spatula until just combined. Transfer to a mixing bowl. Clean and fully dry the stand mixer bowl and whisk.

14. Whip the cream: In the stand mixer fitted with the whisk (or in a large bowl with a hand mixer), whip the heavy cream and vanilla seeds (or extract) on medium-high speed until soft peaks form.

15. Chill the mascarpone cream: Fold the whipped cream into the mascarpone mixture until just combined. Do not overmix, as the mixture will deflate. Cover with plastic wrap pressed against the surface to prevent a skin from forming and chill in the fridge until ready to assemble the tiramisu.

recipe continues

MAKE THE COFFEE SYRUP

16. When ready to assemble, in a small bowl, stir together the hot freshly brewed coffee, sugar, orange zest, and amaretto (if using) until the sugar has dissolved. Use immediately.

ASSEMBLE THE TIRAMISU

17. Cut the fully cooled biscuit cuillère sheet in half lengthwise so you have 2 even rectangles that are about 9 × 13 inches (23 × 33 cm) each.

18. Place one rectangle of biscuit cuillère at the bottom of a 9 × 13-inch (23 × 33 cm) glass* or ceramic baking dish at least 2½ inches (6.5 cm) deep. Using a pastry brush, brush a generous amount of the hot coffee syrup across the surface of the cake until it is well soaked and you don't see any white spots remaining on the surface or the sides of the cake.

Using a glass baking dish here helps so you can see how well the cake has been soaked with the syrup!

19. Spread an even layer of mascarpone cream across the soaked cake. Repeat this process once more, placing the remaining cake layer on top, brushing with the coffee soak, and topping with mascarpone cream.

20. Dust the tiramisu with a layer of cocoa powder using a sifter or small fine-mesh sieve.

21. Chill the tiramisu: Refrigerate until serving time. Serve by scooping out portions with a large spoon.

STORAGE

Best enjoyed the day of assembly. To store, cover gently with plastic wrap and keep in the refrigerator for 1 to 2 days.

BURNT SUGAR ICE CREAM

EVERYONE IN THE food industry has a story about Anthony Bourdain, who was simply Tony to those who knew him. And though I didn't know him very well, my favorite moment with him was the time we spent talking about heartbreak. He was filming a series about craftsmanship and he came over to our kitchens to see what I was working on. At that moment, I was experimenting with an ice cream dish that played with fire. It tasted like a caramel that had sat maybe one minute too long over a stove, and intentionally so. I loosely wrapped a thin strip of paper around a ball of ice cream covered in petals made out of meringue. The dish started off looking like a flower, but when the paper was lit on fire, the flames would slowly work themselves around in a circle and melt the flower petals one by one. What started off beautiful looked like an ashtray at the end. I named the dish "the heartbreak."

Not having a sweet tooth, Tony never really ordered dessert at the end of his meals. "You don't want to know about my heartbreaks, man," he said. "They were a living hell."

We talked a lot about food being a source of comfort in our lives during the tougher times. Not because we were stuffing ourselves with ice cream after a breakup or stress eating, but because it was an art form that brought us joy. Food heals and delights; it nourishes your soul. And when your favorite restaurant closes and you never get to taste that dish you loved again, it can feel like a breakup. Similarly, tasting something familiar is like seeing an old friend. Food is a trigger for memory.

When news came out that Tony had passed away, the whole food world mourned. And I thought back to us talking about heartbreak and food. I'll never forget what he said when at last he took a bite of the ice cream: "I feel better about the world." Then he smiled. "I'm gonna go home and make a mixtape."

MAKES 1 QUART (1 LITER)

INGREDIENTS

Dry Caramel

200 grams	1 cup	sugar

Crème Anglaise Ice Cream Base

530 grams	2¼ cups + 2 tablespoons	whole milk
170 grams	¾ cup	heavy cream
100 grams	5 large	egg yolks
5 grams	2 teaspoons	fleur de sel or Maldon sea salt

EQUIPMENT

Baking sheet	Silicone spatula
Silicone baking mat or parchment paper	Whisk
Mixing bowls	Fine-mesh sieve
Medium saucepan	Ice cream maker

MAKE THE DRY CARAMEL

1. Line a baking sheet with a silicone baking mat or parchment paper.

2. Pour the sugar into a small bowl and set it near the stove. Set a medium sauce-pan over medium heat. When the pan is hot, sprinkle a thin, even layer of sugar over the bottom of the pan. As the sugar melts and caramelizes, slowly sprinkle in more sugar, one small handful at a time, gently stirring with a silicone spatula and making sure each handful has reached an amber brown color before sprin-kling in another handful.* Once all the sugar has been added, cook until it has turned golden amber brown, 1 to 2 minutes. Remove from the heat immediately to keep it from burning and pour the caramel immediately onto the prepared baking sheet in one even layer.

 * *You can move the pot on and off the heat to control the temperature and make sure your sugar doesn't burn and instead stays a golden amber brown.*

recipe continues

3. Let the caramel cool to room temperature, until it has fully hardened, 10 to 15 minutes. Using the back of a spoon, break the caramel into small pieces (about the size of small potato chips). Set aside.

MAKE THE CRÈME ANGLAISE ICE CREAM BASE

4. Make the milk/caramel mixture: In a medium pot, combine the milk, cream, and caramel pieces and bring to a simmer over medium heat, stirring occasionally with a whisk and making sure the caramel is fully melted and incorporated. Remove from the heat.

5. Temper the eggs: In a bowl, whisk together the egg yolks until smooth. While whisking, slowly pour one-third of the warm milk mixture in until fully incorporated to temper the yolks (bringing up the temperature slowly so that the eggs don't scramble). Whisk in another one-third of the milk, then return the egg mixture to the pan with the remainder of the milk mixture and whisk to combine.

6. Make the crème anglaise: Cook the custard over medium heat, stirring constantly with a silicone spatula, until it's thick enough to coat the back of the spatula,* 6 to 8 minutes. Remove from the heat. Stir in the sea salt.

If you can swipe your finger through the custard on the back of the spatula and the line left by your finger remains, it's ready!

7. Chill the crème anglaise: Fill a large bowl with ice and water. Strain the crème anglaise through a fine-mesh sieve into a medium bowl and place the bowl in the ice water. Slowly whisk the crème anglaise until chilled.*

I like to refrigerate the crème anglaise overnight to intensify the caramel flavor, though this is optional and you can make the ice cream right away once the anglaise has cooled. If chilling overnight, cover the bowl with plastic wrap pressed against the surface of the custard to prevent a skin from forming.

8. Make the ice cream: Pour the crème anglaise into an ice cream maker and churn according to the manufacturer's instructions. Transfer the finished ice cream to an airtight 1-quart (1 l) container and freeze until hardened to your liking before serving.

9. Scoop and serve with any of your favorite toppings.

STORAGE

To store, place in an airtight container and keep in the freezer for up to 4 weeks.

PROFITEROLES

I HAVE NEVER been on a diet. In fact, growing up poor it was difficult sometimes to have enough food on the table toward the end of the month. So when I first learned about "cheat days" from "X," I was skeptical.

X was a professional actor, whom many of you would recognize if I disclosed his name. For the roles that he played, it was crucial to stay fit, which led him from one diet to another—high-protein to keto to paleo to one that consisted only of smoothies.

"The logic behind cheat days is that if you allow yourself one day a week to not follow the rules, then ultimately you have less risk of falling off the wagon completely or bingeing," he explained. I gave him a suspicious grin.

From Monday to Saturday, X would come into the bakery, order a cup of black coffee, and window-shop the pastries in the case. Then on Sundays, he'd actually eat. And boy did he eat! Pain au chocolat lightly warmed up, lemony madeleines dusted in powdered sugar, and gooey chocolate chip cookies just to start.

But one Sunday he didn't order anything. Instead, he wanted a recipe. He was celebrating a new role he had landed with an ultimate cheat day. The twist: he would be cooking the full meal at home. No more breadless burgers or butter-free sauces. And the pièce de résistance would be profiteroles.

Each mini choux dough ball—so named because *choux* means "cabbages" in French and that's what the cream puffs look like—would be filled with vanilla ice cream and then topped with a generous pour of molten chocolate sauce. "It's the closest thing to a Champagne tower in dessert form," he said.

I gave him our recipe for profiteroles and some tips for piping and baking. Profiteroles are fun to make because you work the dough over the stove to dry it out and then add as many eggs as you can. You can also save the leftover dough for a few days to make éclairs, gougères, or even crullers. Before he left, I remembered to ask: "What role are you playing?"

He smiled. "Believe it or not, it's a role as a chef."

MAKES 25 TO 30 PROFITEROLES

INGREDIENTS

Pâte à Choux

75 grams	⅓ cup + 1 tablespoon	water
70 grams	¼ cup + 1 teaspoon	whole milk
75 grams	5½ tablespoons	unsalted butter, at room temperature
3 grams	1 teaspoon	sugar
2 grams	1 teaspoon	salt
100 grams	⅔ cup	all-purpose flour
150 to 200 grams	3 to 4 large	eggs

Egg Wash

50 grams	1 large	egg
20 grams	1 large	egg yolk

Pastry Cream

564 grams	1 recipe	Pastry Cream (recipe follows)

Chocolate Sauce

400 grams	1⅔ cups	whole milk
280 grams	2¼ cups	roughly chopped dark chocolate (at least 60% cacao)

EQUIPMENT

Baking sheet	Piping bags
Silicone baking mat or parchment	Plain round piping tips (at least ⅓ inch/1 cm in diameter)
Medium saucepan	Small bowl
Silicone spatula	Pastry brush
Stand mixer	Heatproof bowl

MAKE THE PÂTE À CHOUX DOUGH

1. Position a rack in the center of the oven and preheat the oven to 285°F (140°C). Line a baking sheet with a silicone baking mat or parchment paper.

2. Cook the flour mixture: In a medium saucepan, combine the water, milk, butter, sugar, and salt and bring to a boil over medium heat, stirring occasionally. Add the flour and stir vigorously with a silicone spatula until a dough comes together, a few minutes. Cook, stirring, until a thin film starts to form at the bottom of the saucepan from the dough sticking, 1 to 2 minutes. Keep going until a white film completely covers the bottom of the pan, which should take about 5 more minutes. Remove from the heat.

3. Add the eggs: Transfer the dough to the bowl of a stand mixer fitted with the paddle. With the mixer on medium speed, paddle the dough for 4 to 5 minutes to let off some heat and steam. Then begin to add the eggs one at a time, mixing until each egg is fully incorporated before adding the next one. You'll add 150 to 200 grams of eggs (3 to 4 large eggs).* The outside of the bowl should be hot to the touch, but bearable.

  * *When making pâte à choux, the number of eggs needed will vary. The consistency of the dough dictates how many eggs should be added. Sometimes the dough dries out a bit more in the pan and can take on more eggs. To check, stick a spatula into the dough and lift it high above the bowl. The dough should fall slowly off the spatula in ribbons. It should feel thick, but fluid enough to pipe.*

4. Pipe the dough: Using a spatula, place two large scoops of the warm choux dough into a piping bag fitted with a large plain tip (at least ⅓ inch/1 cm in diameter), filling it one-third full. Push the dough down toward the tip of the bag. Holding the piping bag at a 90-degree angle about ½ inch (1.3 cm) above the prepared baking sheet, pipe rounds of choux dough about 1½ inches (4 cm) in diameter, spacing them about 1 inch (2.5 cm) apart. Gently smooth/flatten the pointed tips of the rounds with your fingers.

recipe continues

MAKE THE EGG WASH

5. In a small bowl, beat together the whole egg and egg yolk. Using a pastry brush (or the tips of your fingers), lightly brush the egg wash over the choux.

6. Bake the choux: Bake the choux until golden brown, light to the touch, and hollow when broken open, 30 to 35 minutes, rotating the pan front to back halfway through. Let the choux fully cool on the pan.

7. Meanwhile, make the pastry cream: Make the pastry cream and chill as directed.

8. Once the choux are fully cooled, gently lift and remove them from the parchment.

9. Fill the choux: Remove the chilled pastry cream from the fridge. Temper the cream (it will have hardened a bit in the fridge) by mixing it with a spatula until it softens and becomes smooth and spreadable. Using a rubber spatula, place two big scoops of pastry cream into a piping bag. Snip off the very tip of piping bag so the opening is about ¼ inch (6 mm) in diameter. Use the tip of the piping bag (or a small paring knife) to pierce a hole into the bottom of a choux, then press on the bag to fill it with pastry cream. Continue until you've filled all the choux.

MAKE THE CHOCOLATE SAUCE

10. In a medium pot, bring the milk to a simmer over medium heat, stirring occasionally. Do not boil.

11. Melt the chocolate: Place the chopped dark chocolate in a heatproof bowl. Pour the warm milk over the chocolate and let it sit for a few minutes to melt the chocolate. Blend with an immersion blender (or stir with a silicone spatula) until well combined and smooth. Use immediately while the sauce is melted and pourable.

12. To serve: Arrange a few profiteroles per serving on a plate or in a shallow bowl. Drizzle the warm chocolate sauce over the top.

STORAGE

Best enjoyed immediately. Unfilled choux can be stored in an airtight container in the refrigerator for up to 1 day. Leftover pastry cream can be stored in the refrigerator wrapped tightly with plastic wrap touching the surface.

PASTRY CREAM

MAKES 564 GRAMS (ENOUGH TO FILL 30 TO 40 PROFITEROLES)

INGREDIENTS

267 grams	1 cup + 3 tablespoons	whole milk
82 grams	6½ tablespoons	sugar #1
82 grams	6½ tablespoons	sugar #2
24 grams	4¼ teaspoons	cornstarch
92 grams	5 large	egg yolks
54 grams	4 tablespoons	unsalted butter, at room temperature, cubed

EQUIPMENT

Medium pot	Large Bowl
Whisk	Fine-mesh sieve

1. Heat the milk and sugar: In a medium pot over medium heat, bring the milk and sugar #1 to a boil, whisking continuously. Remove from the heat.

2. In a large bowl, whisk together the sugar #2 and the cornstarch. Slowly whisk in ½ cup of the warm milk mixture.

3. Temper the egg yolks: While whisking, add the egg yolks one at a time, making sure each yolk is incorporated before adding the next.* Pour the tempered egg yolk mixture back into the pan with the remaining milk mixture and whisk until evenly combined.

recipe continues

This process is called tempering, a cooking technique used to gradually raise the temperature of a cold or room-temperature ingredient (in this case, egg yolks) by adding small amounts of hot liquid, to prevent the cold ingredient from cooking too quickly. If you added all the hot liquid into the eggs at once, you'd end up with scrambled eggs.

4. Cook the pastry cream: Over low to medium heat, while whisking constantly, cook the pastry cream until it noticeably thickens to a pudding-like consistency, about 5 minutes. It will continue to thicken as it cools, so remove it from the heat before too much water has evaporated.

5. Whisk in the butter: Add the cubed butter and whisk until evenly combined, and the pastry cream is pale yellow with a smooth and glossy texture. (Strain through a fine-mesh sieve if needed to help remove any lumps.)

6. Chill the pastry cream: Cover with plastic wrap directly pressed onto the surface to prevent a skin from forming and let it fully cool in the fridge, at least 1 to 2 hours.

STORAGE

Pastry cream can be kept in the refrigerator, covered with plastic wrap directly pressed onto the surface to prevent a skin from forming, for up to 1 day.

STRAWBERRY & FINANCIER FRUIT TART

THE LAST HOUR of the bakery is usually a quiet time. And that's when one of our regulars, Steve, would come in. Steve was in his eighties, always courteous and neatly dressed. He would walk the length of our pastry case in delight and let us know he was picking up dessert after dinner for him and his wife. Most of the time, he would settle on a fruit tart—his wife's favorite—tell everyone he appreciated the great job we were all doing, and delicately carry his box home. Steve was hands down one of the team's favorite patrons.

Our other favorite patron was a woman in her seventies who came by every morning for breakfast. She used to buy a small loaf of financier, a nutty and eggy cake similar to a pound cake. She was toasting it up for her husband for breakfast, she said. It was always pleasant when Marina was here.

When we celebrated the bakery turning one year old, we were excited to invite all our favorite guests to celebrate with us. And to our surprise, Steve and Marina walked in holding hands. For an entire year we had no clue that the two were actually husband and wife. We had always seen them at different times of the day.

When it came time for their sixtieth anniversary, both of them reached out (this time together) for the bakery to do a little cake. "Something simple, just for the two of us," they said.

It instantly hit us that we should make a dessert that perfectly combined their two regular orders. A strawberry tart that had a secret surprise—a slice of financier pound cake lightly soaked in syrup in the middle. Inspired by the first and last meals of the day, the culinary bookends of their daily life. And from that day onward, I always loved hiding a little slice of cake inside a fruit tart. It adds a different texture and also helps absorb some of the juices and jams. It's almost as if the cake and the tart, like Steve and Marina, were made for each other.

MAKES ONE 9-INCH (23 CM) TART (SERVES 6 TO 8)

INGREDIENTS

Pastry Cream

564 grams	1 recipe	Pastry Cream (page 127)

Strawberry Jam

350 grams	3 cups	fresh strawberries, hulled and quartered
80 grams	⅓ cup	granulated sugar #1
20 grams	2 tablespoons	granulated sugar #2
12 grams	1 tablespoon + 1¼ teaspoons	powdered apple pectin

Vanilla Sablé Tart Shell

186 grams	1¼ cups + 1 tablespoon	all-purpose flour
84 grams	⅔ cup	powdered sugar
49 grams	5 tablespoons + 2 teaspoons	cornstarch, sifted
1 gram	¼ teaspoon	salt

Vanilla seeds (scraped from ½ vanilla bean) or ¼ teaspoon vanilla extract

132 grams	1 stick + 1 tablespoon + 1 teaspoon (4.7 oz)	unsalted butter, at room temperature, cubed
49 grams	1 large	egg

Brown Sugar Financier

63 grams	½ cup + 2 tablespoons	almond flour
2 grams	¾ teaspoon	baking powder
60 grams	¼ cup + 3 tablespoons	all-purpose flour
163 grams	6 large	egg whites
109 grams	½ cup packed + 2 tablespoons	dark brown sugar
88 grams	6½ tablespoons	unsalted butter, melted

For Finishing

All-purpose flour, for dusting

Softened butter, for the tart ring

3 to 4 cups fresh strawberries,* hulled and sliced

* Or other fresh berries and fruits of your choice.

EQUIPMENT

Mixing bowls

Whisk

Medium pot

Rubber spatula

Rolling pin

9-inch (23 cm) tart ring or tart pan with a removable bottom

Small paring knife

Parchment paper or silicone baking mat

MAKE THE PASTRY CREAM (THE DAY BEFORE)

1. Make and chill the pastry cream as directed.

MAKE THE STRAWBERRY JAM (THE DAY BEFORE)

2. Macerate the strawberries: In a bowl, combine the strawberries and granulated sugar #1. Toss to evenly coat the berries in sugar, cover the bowl with plastic wrap, and chill in the fridge overnight.

3. Remove the bowl of strawberries from the fridge. In a separate small bowl, whisk together granulated sugar #2 and the pectin until evenly combined.

4. Cook the jam: Transfer the strawberries to a medium pot, cover, and bring to a simmer over low heat. Once there's liquid that starts to release from the strawberries, increase the heat to medium and sprinkle the sugar-pectin mixture evenly over the strawberries and stir until incorporated. (Make sure to sprinkle the pectin mixture evenly, or it will clump.) Cook, stirring occasionally and adjusting the heat as needed if the mixture looks like it's about to boil over, until the strawberries have broken down and the mixture is thick and jammy, 20 to 25 minutes (if you see there's still a bit of liquid remaining, cook for a bit longer).

recipe continues

5. Chill the jam: Remove from the heat. Transfer to a bowl, cover with plastic wrap pressed against the surface to prevent a skin from forming, and chill fully in the fridge until ready to assemble the tart.

MAKE THE VANILLA SABLÉ TART SHELL

6. Make the dough: In a large bowl, combine the all-purpose flour, powdered sugar, cornstarch, salt, and vanilla seeds (or extract). Add the butter and mix with your hands until combined and the butter pieces are the size of tiny peas. (You can also use a stand mixer with the paddle attachment or a hand mixer here.) Add the egg and mix with a rubber spatula until fully incorporated and smooth. Do not overmix.

7. Chill the dough: Remove the dough from the bowl, gently shape it into a ball, and cover with plastic wrap. Flatten into a disc with your hands, then refrigerate for about 30 minutes, until the dough is cold but still pliable (think: texture of clay).* As the dough is chilling, make the financier batter.

* Flattening the dough helps it to chill faster in the fridge. You'll want to make sure the dough is cold before rolling it out. Working with dough that's too warm will cause the tart shell to shrink as it's baking.

MAKE THE BROWN SUGAR FINANCIER

8. Make the batter: In a large bowl, combine the almond flour, baking powder, and all-purpose flour with a whisk. Gradually add the egg whites a little at a time and mix, making sure each addition is fully incorporated before adding the next, scraping down the sides of the bowl with a rubber spatula as needed, until combined.

9. In a small bowl, combine the brown sugar and melted butter with a whisk, breaking up any clumps until smooth.

10. Pour the brown sugar mixture into the flour mixture, and mix until combined. Set aside.

11. Position a rack in the center of the oven and preheat the oven to 330°F (165°C).

recipe continues

12. Roll out the dough: Flour a work surface and rolling pin. Unwrap the disc of chilled dough and transfer it to the work surface. Roll it out into a rectangle about ⅛ inch (3 mm) thick.* Make sure to work fast so the dough doesn't get too warm.

  * If you find that your rolling pin is sticking to the dough, add some more flour. Then roll out the dough between two sheets of parchment paper. The parchment will help when lifting the rolled-out dough onto the sheet pan later on.

13. Cut the dough: Using a 9-inch (23 cm) tart ring as a guide and a paring knife, cut the dough into one large round that's about 2 inches (5 cm) wider than the outside of the ring, so that the dough will be big enough to come up the sides of the tart ring.*

  * Don't throw out your dough scraps! Try sprinkling them with cinnamon sugar and baking them for buttery sugar cookies, or bake them off and crumble them onto your ice cream or morning yogurt.

14. Now the fun part: You're going to "fonçage" the tart dough, or form it into a tart shape in the tart ring. (Don't worry, it's not as intimidating as it sounds!) You can either use a tart ring set on a sheet pan lined with parchment or a silicone baking mat, or a tart pan with a removable bottom. If you're using the tart ring (without a base) as I do, first line a sheet pan with parchment paper and place the tart ring at the center (no need to do this if you're using a tart pan with a bottom).

15. Line the tart ring or pan: Butter the inside of the tart ring or tart pan. Place the dough round on top of the tart ring or pan and push down gently with your fingers, pressing the dough along the inside of the ring or pan and into the inside edge. Don't press too hard and try to keep the dough an even thickness so that it bakes evenly. Use a paring knife to trim any excess dough hanging over the sides of the ring or pan. If your dough is starting to feel warm and lose its shape, return it to the fridge for 15 minutes. Remember, warm or overworked dough will shrink as it bakes. If the dough is still cool to the touch, you can bake it right away.

recipe continues

16. Add the batter: Pour a thin layer of the financier batter into the base of the tart so it's about one-quarter of the way full. Use a rubber spatula to smooth and spread the batter out evenly.

17. Bake the tart shell: Bake until the tart shell is a light golden sandy color* and you don't see any wet spots in the financier layer, 30 to 40 minutes. Let cool for 5 to 10 minutes.

  * *A proper tart shell should be uniformly thin and crispy, with smooth, clean edges and no bubbles and a golden sandy brown color. When you bite into it, it'll disintegrate in your mouth as you chew. Tart shells can be baked in advance, but don't fill them with your creams and fillings too far in advance. Ideally, it's filled and served right away, so the shell stays nice and crispy.*

18. Unmold the tart shell while it's still warm (it'll be easier to remove the ring this way). If you're using a tart pan with a removable bottom, you can push the bottom through with a pint container so it easily unmolds. Let cool completely at room temperature until ready to use.*

  * *Always make sure your tart shell is fully cooled before you start assembling any jam- or cream-based tart. If the shell is still too hot or warm when you pipe in your jam or pastry cream, you'll end up with a soggy-bottomed tart.*

19. Assemble the tart: Spread a thin layer of the cooled strawberry jam across the base of the tart shell, on top of the financier layer. (You can also use a small piping bag to evenly pipe in the jam.)

20. Add the pastry cream: Remove the chilled pastry cream from the fridge. Temper the cream (it will have hardened a bit in the fridge) by mixing it with a spatula until it softens and becomes smooth and spreadable. Fill the tart fully with pastry cream using a spatula or piping bag, leveling it off with a spatula so you have a smooth and flat surface.

21. Top with fruit: Fill the top of the tart with sliced fresh strawberries, starting on the outer edge of the tart shell and working your way inward in a spiral. Serve immediately, using a serrated knife to slice with a gentle sawing motion (rather than pressing down), to avoid crushing or breaking the sides of the tart shell.

STORAGE

Best enjoyed fresh the day of assembly. To store, cover loosely with plastic wrap or place in an airtight container and keep in the refrigerator for up to 2 days.

STONE FRUIT & PASSION FRUIT CURD TRIFLE

REMEMBER THAT EPISODE of *Friends* when Rachel tried to make an English trifle, but the pages of her cookbook got stuck together so the trifle recipe blended with that of a shepherd's pie, and she ended up making a dessert disaster—fruits, pastry cream, and beef—that everyone pretended to like?

Whenever people ask me for a fun group baking project, I think about that episode. And while I would not recommend adding beef to any dessert, layering different flavors of ingredients together to create something unified is the perfect project to make among friends. In my experience, few people can come out of a cooking project *not* as friends. There's magic in spending time around a prep table, coordinating steps and mixing ingredients. And there's time and patience in waiting for the final product to be complete before digging into the feast.

So one holiday season when I was doing a cooking class for a family that was self-described as "having a lot of family drama," it instantly came to me that they should be building a trifle. Each pair would be in charge of a layer, whether it was custard or jam or cake. And then together they would assemble it into a masterpiece. Some executed the recipe perfectly. One pair may have slightly overbaked their cake. Certain fruits weren't as ripe as they should be. But the beauty of the trifle is that each layer harmonizes with the others, so the smaller imperfections from one particular component become barely detectable. Its strength is in the combination. (Well, except when one of those layers is minced meat.)

INGREDIENTS

Chiffon Cake

165 grams	9 large	egg yolks
92 grams	¼ cup + 3 tablespoons	sugar #1
160 grams	1 cup + 3 tablespoons	Japanese Nisshin Violet Komugiko pastry flour*
80 grams	¼ cup + 7 teaspoons	olive oil
114 grams	½ cup	whole milk
275 grams	9 large	egg whites
114 grams	½ cup + 1 tablespoon	sugar #2

This recipe works best with this Japanese pastry flour, which is very light and has a lower gluten content, and is available online and in many Asian supermarkets.

Passion Fruit Curd

4 grams	2 teaspoons	unflavored gelatin powder
22 grams	2 tablespoons	water
106 grams	⅓ cup + 2 tablespoons	passion fruit puree or juice
71 grams	¼ cup + 4 teaspoons	sugar #1
141 grams	3 large	eggs
71 grams	¼ cup + 4 teaspoons	sugar #2
86 grams	6½ tablespoons	unsalted butter, at room temperature

Vanilla Whipped Cream

500 grams	2 cups + 2 tablespoons	heavy cream, well chilled*
50 grams	¼ cup	sugar

Vanilla seeds (scraped from 1 vanilla bean) or ½ tablespoon vanilla extract

Make sure your cream is cold. If it's room temperature or warm, it won't whip up into fluffy peaks.

Assembly

4 pounds stone fruits (peaches, nectarines, apricots, plums, and pluots), pitted and sliced into thin wedges

EQUIPMENT

Stand mixer (or hand mixer)	Offset spatula
Large bowl	Small bowl
Rubber spatula	Medium saucepan
12-cup Bundt pan	Whisk
Wire rack	Serrated knife
Baking sheet	Large glass bowl or trifle bowl

MAKE THE CHIFFON CAKE

1. Position a rack in the center of the oven and preheat the oven to 340°F (170°C).

2. Beat the egg yolks and sugar: In a stand mixer fitted with the whisk, combine the egg yolks and sugar #1 (¼ cup + 3 tablespoons/92 g) and mix on high speed until thick and fluffy, 2 to 3 minutes.

3. Add the flour, oil, and milk: Turn the mixer down to medium-low speed and gradually add the pastry flour a little at a time while continuing to mix, until just combined. Add the olive oil and milk and mix until combined. Transfer the batter to a large bowl. Wash and fully dry the stand mixer bowl and whisk attachment.

4. Make the meringue: In the stand mixer, whip the egg whites on high speed until they're foamy, then slowly add sugar #2 (½ cup + 1 tablespoon/114 g) a little at a time until the mixture reaches medium-stiff peaks.

5. Fold in the meringue: Gently fold the meringue into the batter in three additions with a rubber spatula, making sure each addition is incorporated before adding the next, until the mixture is just combined. Do not overmix, as you don't want to deflate the fluffy meringue texture.

recipe continues

6. Bake the cake: Pour the batter into a 12-cup Bundt pan until it reaches three-quarters full (you will have some excess batter remaining). Bake until the cake is lightly golden brown and a cake tester inserted in the center comes out clean, 40 to 45 minutes.

7. Cool and unmold the cake: Place a wire rack on a baking sheet. Remove the cake from the oven and carefully invert the pan onto the wire rack. Let the cake fully cool upside down in the pan, about 1 hour. Once cooled, carefully unmold the cake, using an offset spatula to pull it away from the sides if needed.

MAKE THE PASSION FRUIT CURD

8. In a small bowl, combine the gelatin and water and whisk until dissolved. Set aside.

9. In a medium saucepan, combine the passion fruit puree and sugar #1 (¼ cup + 4 teaspoons/71 g) and bring to a simmer over medium heat. Do not boil. Remove from the heat.

10. In a bowl, whisk together the eggs and sugar #2 (¼ cup + 4 teaspoons/71 g) until evenly combined.

11. Temper the eggs: Pour one-third of the warm passion fruit mixture into the egg mixture, whisking until smooth. Repeat with another one-third of the passion fruit mixture, mix until combined, then pour this tempered egg mixture back into the pan with the remaining passion fruit mixture and whisk until smooth and combined.

12. Cook the curd: Set the pan over medium heat and cook the curd, stirring continuously, until it starts to bubble. Remove from the heat and let cool until just warm.

13. Finish the curd: Add the butter and gelatin mixture to the curd and whisk until fully incorporated and the curd is silky and smooth. Transfer to a bowl. Cover with plastic wrap that touches the surface to prevent a skin from forming and let cool completely in the fridge before assembling the trifle.

MAKE THE VANILLA WHIPPED CREAM

14. In a stand mixer fitted with the whisk (or in a large bowl with a hand mixer), whisk the heavy cream, sugar, and vanilla seeds (or extract) on high speed until soft peaks form, just a few minutes.

ASSEMBLE THE TRIFLE

15. Using a serrated knife,* gently cut the cooled chiffon cake into cubes.

> *A serrated knife works well here, so you don't crush the fluffy cake when cutting.*

16. Remove the chilled passion fruit curd from the fridge. If it's firm, use a rubber spatula to mix until it's soft and spreadable.

17. Place a layer of cubed chiffon cake at the bottom of a large glass bowl or trifle bowl. Add a layer of the cooled passion fruit curd on top, followed by vanilla whipped cream and mixed stone fruit wedges. Repeat this process once more, and finish with more stone fruits on top. Serve right away.

STORAGE

Best enjoyed the day of assembly. To store, cover gently with plastic wrap and keep in the refrigerator for 1 to 2 days.

RASPBERRY ROSE SOUFFLÉ

WHEN IT COMES to baking, few desserts incite as much fear as the soufflé. A true diva, the soufflé waits for no one. It demands you place your order *before* you eat your main course. But that was the dish that Kevin wanted to make for his "promposal." Kevin was seventeen years old and out to impress. He walked into the bakery one day and declared he was a longtime supporter and now he needed our help in return. His best friend, the object of his affection, had waited in line with him at the bakery in one of their first memories together, and now he was hoping she'd go with him to the most important dance of his life.

Kevin had been practicing his soufflé recipe at home but couldn't get it perfect—and it needed to be perfect. Sometimes he opened his oven too soon and the soufflé deflated. Other times he took it out from the oven too quickly. But his young heart kept trying. As prom tickets started to go on sale, Kevin came into the store in a panic as his soufflé was still deflating. Four emails to our inbox and numerous phone calls asking to speak with me later, Kevin and I finally met when he stopped me next to my car as I was leaving work one day.

At first, I couldn't understand why he was worried. But as I heard him pour his heart out, I smiled. I let him in on my secret to all soufflés: I use a bit of cornstarch to make it more resilient than the traditional soufflé recipe. And my favorite type of soufflé is actually a fruit one made with raspberries and just a dash of rose water. I find it more refreshing and lighter than the chocolate ones.

A few days later, Kevin sent me a photo of his success. "I hope you also took photos of all those failed attempts," I responded, "because that's what truly made your promposal a special one—that even in failure you tried again and again." Persistence in all things, especially in cooking, is what makes a great chef.

His prom date said yes.

INGREDIENTS

Vanilla Rose Crème Anglaise

265 grams	1 cup + 2 tablespoons	whole milk
85 grams	¼ cup + 2 tablespoons	heavy cream
Vanilla seeds (scraped from ½ vanilla bean) or ¼ teaspoon vanilla extract		
50 grams	3 large	egg yolks
65 grams	⅓ cup	sugar
1 to 2 drops rose water or rose extract		

Soufflé

250 grams	8 ounces	fresh raspberries
Unsalted butter and sugar, for the ramekins		
250 grams	1 cup	whole milk
25 grams	5 teaspoons	water
25 grams	1 tablespoon + 1¼ teaspoons	cornstarch
160 grams	5 large	egg whites
100 grams	½ cup	sugar

EQUIPMENT

Medium pot	Pastry brush
Whisk	Stand mixer (or hand mixer)
Mixing bowls	Rubber spatula
Silicone spatula	Piping bag
Baking sheet	Offset spatula
8 ceramic ramekins, 3½ inches (9 cm) in diameter and 2 inches (5 cm) deep	

MAKE THE VANILLA ROSE CRÈME ANGLAISE

1. Make the warm milk mixture: In a medium pot, combine the milk, cream, and vanilla seeds (or extract) and bring to a simmer over medium heat, stirring occasionally with a whisk. Remove from the heat.

2. Make the egg yolk mixture: In a bowl, whisk together the egg yolks and sugar until fully combined.

3. Temper the egg yolk mixture: While whisking, slowly pour one-third of the warm milk mixture into the egg yolk mixture and whisk until fully incorporated to temper the eggs. Whisk in another one-third of the milk mixture, then pour the tempered egg mixture back into the pot with the remaining milk mixture, stirring until combined.

4. Make the crème anglaise: Cook the custard over medium heat, stirring continuously with a silicone spatula, until it's thick enough to coat the back of the spatula, 4 to 5 minutes. (If you can swipe your finger through the custard on the back of the spatula and the line left by your finger remains, it's ready!). Remove from the heat.

5. Add the rose water and stir until combined.* Chill the anglaise in the fridge until ready to serve.

  * *Rose can be a very strong flavor. Start out with just
    1 to 2 drops, and add more to taste as needed.*

PREPARE THE SOUFFLÉ

6. Freeze the raspberries: Spread out the raspberries on a baking sheet or a plate. Freeze until ready to use.

7. Prepare the ramekins: Have ready 8 ceramic ramekins measuring 3½ inches (9 cm) in diameter and 2 inches (5 cm) deep. Melt a few tablespoons of butter in a small bowl in the microwave. Using a pastry brush, brush a thin, even layer of butter on the base and up the sides of each ramekin. Add a small spoon of sugar and roll it around, turning the ramekin so the sugar coats the sides and base evenly. Tap out any excess. Using the tip of your thumb, clean around the top rim of each ramekin.

8. Make the soufflé batter: In a medium pot, combine the milk, water, and cornstarch and bring to a simmer over medium heat, stirring occasionally with a whisk

recipe continues

until it thickens almost to the consistency of a loose pudding. Remove from the heat. Let cool until just warm.

9. Preheat the oven to 375°F (190°C).

10. Make the meringue: In a stand mixer fitted with the whisk (or in a large bowl with a hand mixer), whip the egg whites on high speed until they're foamy, a few minutes. While continuing to whip on high, gradually add the sugar a few table-spoons at a time, mixing until stiff peaks form.

11. Fold in the meringue: Carefully fold the meringue mixture into the warm milk mixture with a rubber spatula in three additions, until just combined. Make sure not to deflate the air in the egg whites and do not overmix. The first addition can be mixed a bit more vigorously to lighten up the milk mixture, while the last two additions should be folded in very gently.

12. Add the raspberries: Remove the raspberries from the freezer. Gently crush them into small pieces with your hands. Carefully fold the raspberry pieces into the soufflé batter with a rubber spatula until evenly distributed.

13. Pipe the batter into the ramekins: Fill a piping bag with the soufflé batter and snip off the tip to form a large opening, about 1 inch (2.5 cm). Holding the bag over the center of a ramekin, pipe in the batter until it reaches the top edge. Use an offset spatula to smooth out the top of each soufflé so you have a flat, even surface. Repeat with the remaining ramekins. Run your thumb around in-side the top rim of each ramekin, turning the ramekin as you go.*

* This creates a little separation between the soufflé batter and the ramekin, allowing the soufflé to rise up straight and evenly in the oven.

14. Bake the soufflés: Place the ramekins on a baking sheet about 2 inches apart. Bake until they've risen, the surface is just barely light blond, and it's set when you give it a little jiggle, 15 to 20 minutes (the baking time may vary depending on the type of oven you have, so watch carefully). If you see the soufflés start to crack on the sides, they have overbaked. Carefully remove the soufflés from the oven.

15. Transfer each ramekin to a plate.* Use a spoon to make a small hole on top of the soufflé, and pour the cooled vanilla rose crème anglaise over and serve immediately. (Be sure to eat within a few minutes; the longer the soufflés sit out, the more they'll start to deflate.)

  * *You can sprinkle powdered sugar on top of the soufflés at this point, if you wish, before pouring the crème anglaise.*

STORAGE

Best enjoyed immediately. If you have excess batter, pipe it into ramekins and keep in the refrigerator (for no more than a few hours or it will start to deflate) until ready to bake.

HOT CHOCOLATE
WITH PINK CHAMPAGNE MARSHMALLOWS

I HAVE BEEN a part of over a hundred proposals in my lifetime. Pastry chefs stand in that critical time just before the meal ends, when the golden opportunity comes to pop the question. And I've done my fair share of being an accomplice, hiding diamond rings in between bites of chocolate décor. There are often tears of joy. Almost always, there's an element of shock when someone gets down on one knee. And yes, there have been a few times when the answer was no.

Yet among all the lavish and over-the-top proposals, some of my favorites have been quick and sincere. And one of them happened over a small cup of hot chocolate.

The hot chocolate we serve at the bakery comes with a small marshmallow flower that "blooms" when it comes into contact with the heat of the chocolate. And I remember seeing the soon-to-be groom, nervous, holding out a ring in front of me and asking if we could hide it in the marshmallow blossom. Our manager, whose role it was to drop the marshmallow blossom into the chocolate, told me later his hands were trembling out of nervousness. Our team from behind the glass doors saw the gentleman get down on one knee.

There was no fancy-jackets-required restaurant. There were no multicourse menus or Champagne corks popping. It was just a cup of hot chocolate, and a sweet sip to begin a new life together. And it was enough.

MAKES 8 CUPS

INGREDIENTS

Pink Champagne Marshmallows (recipe follows)

1.54 kilograms	6¼ cups	whole milk
400 grams	4 cups	chopped dark chocolate

EQUIPMENT

Medium pot   Whisk

1. Make the marshmallows as directed.

2. In a medium pot, bring the milk to boil while stirring with a whisk. Add the chocolate and whisk until evenly combined and smooth. Return to a boil while continuing to stir. Once boiling, remove from the heat immediately.

3. Pour into mugs and serve immediately with a marshmallow on top of each one.

STORAGE

Best enjoyed right away. To store the hot chocolate, place in an airtight container and keep in the refrigerator for up to 2 days.

PINK CHAMPAGNE MARSHMALLOWS

MAKES 20 TO 30 MARSHMALLOWS

27 grams	3 tablespoons	unflavored gelatin powder
159 grams	⅔ cup	pink champagne
372 grams	1½ cups + ⅓ cup	granulated sugar
340 grams	1 cup	honey
103 grams	½ cup	water
Cooking spray		
Powdered sugar, for dusting		

Small bowl

Medium pot

Whisk

Candy thermometer

Stand mixer

Baking sheet

Silicone baking mat

Rubber or offset spatula

Knife or cookie cutters of your choice

1. Bloom the gelatin: In a small bowl, whisk together the gelatin and pink champagne until the gelatin has dissolved. Let the mixture sit a few minutes until the gelatin has bloomed (when it has absorbed the majority of the liquid, gaining 2 to 3 times its original volume, and feels firm and set).

2. Cook the honey syrup: In a medium pot, combine the granulated sugar, honey, and water and bring to a simmer over medium heat. Stir continuously with a whisk and cook until it reaches 255°F (124°C) on a candy thermometer. Add the gelatin mixture to the pot, stirring until incorporated.

3. Make the meringue: In a stand mixer fitted with the whisk, slowly pour the hot sugar mixture down the side of the bowl while whipping on high speed until stiff peaks form.

4. Set the marshmallows: Line a baking sheet with a silicone baking mat. Spray the surface of the silicone mat with cooking spray. Pour the marshmallow onto the mat, spreading it in one even layer with a rubber or offset spatula. Let the marshmallow firm until it holds its shape.

5. Cut into desired shapes using a knife or cookie cutters. Toss the marshmallows in powdered sugar to prevent them from sticking to one another.

STORAGE

To store the marshmallows, place in an airtight container and keep in a cool dry place on the counter or in the refrigerator for up to 1 week.

CHAPTER 4
Family Life

As we grow and build our family, life extends
far and wide. All of a sudden, there are kids and
picnics, and teachers and mentors—giving us more
reason to bake than ever before.

MEDITATION

PALMIERS

I ALWAYS FIND it a bit ironic when people tell me their favorite pastime is baking. They describe it to me as "meditative" and "relaxing," while in the back of my mind I'm thinking that baking is anything but. In my world, it's a high-pressure and demanding profession. The same can also be said for my friend Christina's profession, which is seen by others as a recreational activity. Christina is a ceramic artist. Over the years she has helped us make beautiful hand-thrown plates for our restaurants. There was one made to look like a dollop of whipped cream, so fragile and refined that I've seen guests attempt to eat it.

Christina once showed me her studio setup and taught me how to gather a small handful of clay and center it on the pottery wheel. She was patient and worked meticulously, never losing the balance of pressure between her fingers. All the similarities between pottery and baking quickly became clear to me. It's repetitive; you are replicating the same motions. There's waiting; things must rest. And funnily enough—they both end with the product being baked off in an "oven."

One of the things that Christina loves to do is make puff pastry—slowly layering the butter and the dough and rolling it out, letting it rest each time in the kitchen. From this one dough, you can make beautiful palmiers, or "elephant ear" cookies, that are perfectly caramelized on the outside with a buttery crunch that slowly melts in your mouth after your first bite.

We laughed that she likes to bake as a hobby, and I wouldn't mind picking up ceramics as something fun to do on the side. Ultimately, though, making a hundred bowls or a hundred cakes feels a lot different than making just one. Yet we completely understood why each of these forms of art has its draw.

When the first pot that I had ever thrown came out of the kiln, Christina sent me a photo to show me the end result. There was a wonky side that didn't look centered.

"It's wabi-sabi," said Christina. "There's beauty in imperfection in ceramics."

I laughed. In pastry, there isn't a word for that.

MAKES 25 TO 30 PALMIERS

INGREDIENTS

Reversed Puff Pastry Dough*

700 grams	5½ cups	all-purpose flour
17 grams	1 tablespoon	salt
300 grams	1¼ cups	cold water
225 grams	2 sticks (8 oz)	unsalted butter, at room temperature

All-purpose flour, for dusting

* You can also use store-bought puff pastry instead, but I always prefer to make my own! If you're using store-bought puff pastry, skip to the Caramel Powder step on page 161 (however, note that because the final size of your puff pastry will be different, the shaping and baking time will differ).

Butter Block for Puff Pastry

| 253 grams | 2 cups | all-purpose flour |
| 506 grams | 4 sticks + 4 tablespoons (18 oz) | unsalted butter, at room temperature |

Caramel Powder

| 400 grams | 2 cups | sugar |

EQUIPMENT

Stand mixer with a dough hook	2 silicone baking mats
Parchment paper	Small bowl
Pencil	Medium saucepan
Ruler	Food processor
Offset spatula	Spray bottle
Rolling pin	Sharp knife
Baking sheet	Small sieve or sifter

MAKE THE REVERSED PUFF PASTRY DOUGH (DAY BEFORE)

1. Mix the dough: In a stand mixer fitted with the dough hook, combine the flour, salt, cold water, and butter. Mix on low speed until just blended, about 2½ minutes. The dough should look rough (since there's been no gluten development at this stage just yet).

2. Chill the dough: Dust a work surface with flour. Shape the dough into a 9-inch (23 cm) square about ⅝ inch (1.5 cm) thick. Cover with plastic wrap and refrigerate until chilled, about 45 minutes. Wash and fully dry the stand mixer bowl.

MAKE THE BUTTER BLOCK FOR THE PUFF PASTRY (DAY BEFORE)

3. Blend the flour and butter: In a stand mixer fitted with the paddle, combine the all-purpose flour and butter. Mix on low speed, stopping to scrape down the sides and bottom of the bowl as needed, until there are no streaks of butter. The mixture should feel like soft and pliable butter.

4. Form the butter block: On a piece of parchment paper, use a pencil and a ruler to draw a 13-inch (33 cm) square. Flip the parchment paper over so the butter won't come into contact with the pencil marks. Place the butter in the center of the square and spread it evenly with an offset spatula to fill the square. Refrigerate for 20 minutes, until firm but still pliable.

5. Remove the butter from the fridge: The butter should still be soft enough to bend slightly without cracking. (If it's too firm, lightly beat it with a rolling pin on a lightly floured surface until it becomes pliable. Make sure to press the butter back into its original 13-inch/33-cm square shape after working it.)

6. Remove the dough from the fridge: Unwrap the chilled dough square and place in the center of the butter block so it looks like a diamond in the center of the square (the corners of the dough facing the center of the butter block sides).

7. Enfold the dough: Fold the corners of the butter block up and over to the center of the dough. The butter block should completely cover the dough.* Pinch the seams of the butter block together to prevent the dough from peeking through.**

recipe continues

* There are two kinds of puff pastry: When the butter is on the inside, it's a regular puff pastry. When the butter is on the outside—like this one—it's a reversed (or inverse) puff pastry, which can result in a flakier and more caramelized pastry, and it's my preference!

** Whenever folding butter, it's important to work quickly to ensure it doesn't melt. It helps if your work surface and kitchen/room are cool.

8. Make the first fold (day before): Generously flour a work surface and rolling pin. You'll need a rather large work surface for this task. With the rolling pin, using steady, even pressure, roll the butter-covered dough out from the center vertically so it triples in length. When finished rolling, you should have a long rectangle about 26 × 11½ inches (66 × 29 cm).*

* Keeping the shape of the dough is very important at this point to ensure even layers.

9. Place the dough so the longer sides run left to right. From the right side, fold one-third of the dough onto itself, keeping the edges lined up with each other. From the left side, fold one-third of the dough on top of the side that has already been folded. Line up all the edges so you're left with an even rectangle.*

* In the lamination process, this is known as a "letter fold," since the dough is being folded as if it were a piece of paper going into an envelope.

10. Rest the dough: Wrap the dough in plastic wrap and refrigerate for 15 to 20 minutes to rest.*

* Resting the dough relaxes the gluten and keeps the butter chilled.

11. Make the second and third folds (day before): Remove the chilled dough from the fridge and unwrap. It should be firm, but not hard. If it's not pliable, let it sit out briefly to soften. Place on a lightly floured work surface, with the open seams at the top and bottom.* With a rolling pin, using steady, even pressure, roll the dough out from the center vertically from top to bottom. The dough should triple in length and increase in width one and a half times; this will take several passes. When finished, you should have a long rectangle that's about 34½ × 13 inches (87 × 33 cm).

*When rolling out dough, it's always best to have the open seams
on the top and bottom (rather than on the left and right sides) to
ensure the layers remain even and don't slide when you are rolling.*

12. Make a double book fold: Rotate the dough so the longer sides now run left to right. This time, from the left side, fold one-quarter of the dough onto itself. From the right side, fold one-quarter of the dough onto itself. The two ends should meet in the middle of the dough. Fold the dough in half where the ends meet.* Wrap the dough again in plastic wrap and refrigerate for 15 to 20 minutes to rest.

13. Remove the chilled dough from the fridge and unwrap. Place on a lightly floured work surface, with the open seams at the top and bottom. Make another double book fold: Once again, roll out the dough until it triples in length and increases in width one and a half times, then rotate the dough so the longer sides now run left to right. Make the double book fold, as above in step 12. Wrap the dough in plastic wrap and refrigerate overnight.

MAKE THE CARAMEL POWDER

14. Make dry caramel: Line a baking sheet with a silicone baking mat or parchment paper. Put the sugar in a small bowl and set it near the stove. Place a medium saucepan over medium heat. When the pan is hot, sprinkle a thin, even layer of sugar over the bottom of the pan. As the sugar melts and caramelizes, slowly sprinkle in more sugar, one small handful at a time, gently stirring with a silicone spatula and making sure each handful has reached an amber brown color before adding another handful.* Once all the sugar has been added, cook until it has turned golden amber brown, 1 to 2 minutes. Remove from the heat immediately to keep it from burning.

*You can move the pan on and off the heat to control
the temperature to make sure your sugar doesn't burn
and instead stays a golden amber brown.*

15. Pour the caramel immediately onto the prepared baking sheet in one even layer. Let cool to room temperature, until it has hardened, 10 to 15 minutes. Using the back of a spoon, break the caramel into small pieces. Place the pieces in a food processor and blitz into a fine powder. Set aside.

recipe continues

16. Roll out the puff pastry (day of): Remove the puff pastry from the fridge and unwrap. Place it on a lightly floured work surface. With a rolling pin, using steady, even pressure, roll the dough out into a rectangle that's about 43 × 15 inches (110 × 38 cm), with the longer sides at the top and bottom. Using a sharp knife, trim the edges so you have straight sides.

17. Fill a spray bottle with water. Lightly spritz the surface of the dough with water, then sprinkle on a handful of caramel powder in one even layer.

18. Starting from the left side, fold one-quarter of the dough onto itself. From the right side, fold one-quarter of the dough onto itself. The two ends should meet in the center of the dough (it will look like an open book). Repeat once more:

From the left side, fold one-quarter of the dough onto itself, then from the right side, fold one-quarter of the dough onto itself, with the two ends meeting in the center (it will look like an even narrower open book). Fold the dough in half along the center seam (the two sides should close like a book). Cover with plastic wrap and freeze until firm.*

* *Chilling allows the dough to firm up so the palmiers are easier to cut. It also helps them puff up better in the oven.*

19. Position a rack in the center of the oven and preheat the oven to 350°F (175°C). Line a baking sheet with a silicone baking mat.

20. Cut the dough into palmiers: Remove the chilled dough from the freezer. Use a sharp knife to cut ½-inch (1.3 cm) slices.* Place the palmiers cut side up on the prepared baking sheet at least 2 to 3 inches (5 to 7.5 cm) apart (these will spread quite a bit). Sprinkle each palmier with a generous layer of caramel powder. Lay another silicone mat on top (this keeps the palmiers flat during baking and prevents the sugar from burning too quickly).

* *If you're not slicing all of the palmier dough here, you can freeze the remaining block of laminated dough to slice and bake later.*

21. Bake the palmiers: Bake for 25 minutes. Remove the upper silicone mat and carefully flip each palmier over with an offset spatula or turner. Place the silicone mat back on top and return to the oven to bake until golden brown and to allow the other side to caramelize evenly, 22 to 25 more minutes.

22. Remove from the oven and remove the top silicone mat. Using a small sieve or sifter, dust the top of each palmier with caramel powder. Return to the oven for 1 minute until the caramel melts. Remove from the oven and let cool completely, so the caramel hardens.

23. Once cool, lift each palmier off the silicone mat and enjoy.

STORAGE

Best enjoyed immediately. To store, place in an airtight container and keep at room temperature for 3 to 4 days.

PASTEIS DE NATA

A LARGE PORTION of my thirties was spent traveling, filled with meals around the world. I have found some of my most memorable eats in some of the most lauded restaurants and on jetlagged convenient-store runs alike. Believe it or not, it is not always in the location where the food was invented that I've had the best version of that item. While I know some would object, in my humble experience, I've had the best sushi of my life in Hong Kong, not Japan. My favorite gelato is in France, not Italy. And the best burger is perhaps in London, not the US.

But there's one place of origin that hands down has the best version of the pastry it also gave birth to—Portugal and the *pasteis de nata*. Were you to travel to Portugal, you would see different generational shops in their own neighborhoods, each with a line out the door. The scent of burnt sugar and custard wafts down the street, and almost every pastry I've had come into my hands was warm and freshly baked. Sprinkled with just the tiniest bit of cinnamon on top, as the locals would do.

When I returned to New York, I was determined to try to replicate it and I called up my good friend and fellow chef George from Portugal to ask if he would share a recipe. I've since adapted it to ingredients I can find here as well as everyday tools you might have at home. It doesn't taste the same without the sound of waves crashing against Belém Tower under the Lisbon sun. But it's got that distinct crunchiness in the shell and a satisfying gooey center. A stand-in until your next trip back.

INGREDIENTS

Pastry Dough

600 grams	4¼ cups	all-purpose flour
320 grams	1½ cups	water
4 grams	2 teaspoons	salt

Butter Block for Pastry Dough

400 grams	3½ sticks (14 oz)	unsalted butter, at room temperature

Custard Filling

750 grams	3 cups + 3 tablespoons	whole milk
600 grams	2¼ cups + 3 tablespoons	heavy cream
4 or 5 cinnamon sticks		
21 grams	3½ tablespoons	grated zest (from 3 lemons)
300 grams	1½ cups	sugar
180 grams	9 large	egg yolks
45 grams	6 tablespoons	all-purpose flour
Butter or cooking spray		
Cinnamon sugar (optional)		

EQUIPMENT

Stand mixer with a dough hook	Rubber spatula
Parchment paper	Whisk
Pencil	Fine-mesh sieve
Ruler	Rolling pin
Offset spatula	24 pasteis de nata molds (about 3 inches/ 7.5 cm in diameter, and ¾ inch/2 cm deep)
Medium pot	

MAKE THE PASTRY DOUGH

1. Mix the dough: In a stand mixer fitted with the dough hook, combine the flour, water, and salt and mix on medium speed until a dough forms. Continue mixing until the dough becomes elastic and pulls away from the sides of the bowl.

2. Chill the dough: Form the dough into a ball and transfer to a large piece of plastic wrap. Wrap the dough and use your hands to flatten it into a disc. Chill in the fridge until cold and firm.

MEANWHILE, MAKE THE BUTTER BLOCK

3. On a piece of parchment paper, use a pencil and ruler to draw an 8-inch (20 cm) square. Flip the parchment paper over so the butter won't come into contact with the pencil marks. Place the butter in the center of the square and spread evenly with an offset spatula to fill the square. Refrigerate for 20 to 30 minutes, until firm but still pliable.

MAKE THE CUSTARD FILLING

4. Infuse the milk mixture: In a medium pot, combine the milk, cream, cinnamon sticks, and lemon zest and bring to a simmer over medium heat while whisking occasionally. Turn off the heat, cover the pot with the lid, and let sit for 20 minutes to allow the cinnamon and lemon to infuse. Use a fine-mesh sieve to strain out the cinnamon sticks and lemon zest.

5. In a mixing bowl, whisk together the sugar and egg yolks until combined. Add the flour and mix until combined.

6. Temper the egg mixture: Pour one-third of the warm milk mixture into the yolk mixture, whisking until combined. Add another one-third of the milk mixture to the yolk mixture, whisking until combined. Pour this all back into the pot with the remaining milk mixture.

7. Cook and cool the custard: Over medium heat, cook the custard until it thickens and bubbles, stirring continuously with a whisk. Transfer the custard to a heatproof bowl. Cover with plastic wrap pressed against the surface to prevent a skin from forming and let cool fully in the fridge.

8. Laminate the dough: Generously flour a work surface and rolling pin. You'll need a rather large work surface for this task. Remove the chilled dough from the fridge and unwrap it. With the rolling pin, using steady, even pressure, roll the dough to a 12½-inch (32 cm) square that's about ¼ inch (6 mm) thick.

recipe continues

9. Remove the butter from the fridge: It should still be soft enough to bend slightly without cracking. (If it's too firm, lightly beat the butter with a rolling pin on a lightly floured surface until it becomes pliable. Make sure to press the butter back to its original 8-inch/20-cm square after working it.)

10. Place the chilled butter block in the center of the dough so it looks like a diamond (rotated 45 degrees, so the corners of the butter point at the center of the dough sides).

11. Enfold the butter: Fold the corners of the dough up and over to the center of the butter block. The dough should completely cover, or "lock in," the butter block. Pinch the seams of the dough together to prevent the butter from peeking through.* (If the dough starts to feel warm, chill in the fridge for 20 to 30 minutes.)

   * *Whenever laminating, it's important to work quickly to ensure the dough doesn't get too warm and the butter doesn't start to melt. It helps if your work surface and kitchen/room are cool.*

12. With the rolling pin, using steady, even pressure, roll the dough out from the center vertically to lengthen and slightly widen and create a rectangle about 16 × 9½ inches (40 × 24 cm).*

   * *Keeping the shape of the dough is very important at this point to ensure even layers.*

13. Make letter fold: Place the dough so the longer sides run left to right. From the right side, fold one-third of the dough onto itself, keeping the edges lined up with each other. From the left side, fold one-third of the dough on top of the side that has already been folded. Line up all the edges so you're left with an even rectangle.*

   * *In the lamination process, this is known as a "letter fold," since the dough is being folded as if it were a piece of paper going into an envelope.*

14. Rest the dough: Wrap the dough in plastic wrap and refrigerate for 15 to 20 minutes to rest.*

Resting the dough relaxes the gluten and keeps the butter chilled.

15. Roll out the dough again: Remove the chilled dough from the fridge and unwrap it. It should be firm, but not hard. If it's not pliable, let it sit out briefly to soften. Place on a lightly floured work surface, with the open seams at the top and bottom. With a rolling pin, using steady, even pressure, roll the dough out from the center vertically from top to bottom to lengthen and slightly widen and once again create a rectangle about 16 × 9½ inches (40 × 24 cm).*

* When rolling out dough, it's always best to have the open seams on the top and bottom (rather than on the left and right sides) to ensure the layers remain even and don't slide when you are rolling.

16. Make a second letter fold and chill: Rotate the dough so the longer sides now run left to right. Once again, from the right side, fold one-third of the dough onto itself, lining up the edges with each other. From the left side, fold one-third of the dough on top of the side that has already been folded. Line up all the edges so you're left with an even rectangle. Wrap the dough and refrigerate for 15 to 20 more minutes.

17. Make a third letter fold and chill: Follow the steps above to roll out the dough (with the open seams at the top and bottom) again and make a third single letter fold. Wrap the dough and chill once more for 15 to 20 more minutes.

18. Form and chill the dough log: Remove the chilled dough from the fridge. Flour a work surface. Using a rolling pin, roll out the dough into a rectangle that's about 15 × 12 inches (38 × 30 cm) and about ⅙ inch (2 mm) thick, with the longer sides on the top and bottom. Starting at the bottom edge, carefully roll the dough up tightly with your fingertips so it forms a long log that's about 1½ inches (4 cm) in diameter. Transfer the log to a parchment-lined baking sheet and place in the freezer to chill until firm.

19. Cut the dough log: Using a sharp knife, cut the log into slices ½ inch (1.3 cm) thick. Cut as many slices as you have pasteis de nata molds. (Any excess dough can be wrapped in plastic and frozen for later use.)

recipe continues

20. Lightly grease your pasteis de nata molds with butter or cooking spray.

21. Roll out and shape the tart shells: Tuck the end/tail of each dough spiral to the bottom and use your hand to press each disc down to flatten. Lightly flour both sides of the dough. Using a rolling pin, roll out to a round that's about 3½ inches (9 cm) in diameter and place it into a prepared mold. Using your fingers, push the dough down into the bottom, edges, and up the sides of the tin to form an even crust. Repeat with the remaining molds.

22. Chill the lined molds: Transfer to the freezer (preferably) or fridge to keep the crusts chilled until ready to fill and bake.

23. Position a rack in the center of the oven and preheat the oven to 550°F (290°C) or the hottest setting for your oven.

24. Fill the tart shells: Ladle or spoon the custard into the molds until they're about 80 percent full (the custard will bubble and puff up a bit in the oven and then fall slightly once cooled). Place them on a baking sheet (you may need two baking sheets).

25. Bake the tarts: Bake until the custard starts to caramelize and blister and the edges of the pastry turn golden brown, 9 to 11 minutes. The bubbles on top will look like they're just about to burn; don't be alarmed, the custard is caramelizing due to the high heat in the oven and this is the sign of a proper pasteis de nata.

26. Cool and unmold: Remove from the oven and let cool in the molds for 15 minutes (be careful, the molds and pastries are very hot; remember they were baked in a 550°F oven!). Then carefully unmold and transfer to a wire rack to cool for a few more minutes.

27. Enjoy while they're still warm (optional: finish with a sprinkle of cinnamon sugar on top).

STORAGE

Best enjoyed immediately.

PINEAPPLE MANGO ICE POPS

SOME DESSERTS ARE time machines. No matter how old we are, they transport us right back to our childhood the moment we taste them. Ice cream and Popsicles are such desserts. When you're eating an ice cream cone or a Popsicle, there's no delicate bite or slow nibble. You hold it in your hand and consume it in continuous steady swoops. No pauses, no breaks. In those fleeting minutes, the frozen delight in front of you is your main focus. It sets the pace.

When we first met our PR director, Jessica, she let us know that her father was an ice cream man. He owned a small shop in New Jersey that he opened and closed daily by himself. And he wouldn't have it any other way. In his thirty-five years there, he gifted free cones to the winning Little League teams and he made scoops for children who grew up and brought their own kids in. Jessica would rave about how when she was growing up her dad brought individual ice cream cups to her school while other kids only had packaged snacks from the convenience store. One year, he made pumpkin ice cream for our team at the bakery, packed it up in a cooler, and drove it over carefully so that we could try it for Thanksgiving. I remember time stopped when he arrived and all of us gathered around the ice cream before it melted.

Jessica's dad passed away unexpectedly one day. Within hours, flowers were lined up in front of his ice cream shop until they were three layers deep. That was right around the time I became a first-time dad and had come to understand the kind of love that would make someone drive hours with precious cargo in his car just so he could give a bite of ice cream to his child, and to the rest of us who are kids at heart.

When my son recently fell and had his first big accident, I was in a state of panic wondering what more seasoned fathers would do. Almost by instinct, I reached for a Popsicle and gave it to him. We had started to make a few Popsicles with purees and juices during the summer to cool off with the kids, and these were a simple mixture of my favorite tropical fruits at their peak ripeness. Soon the tears dried up and the pain subsided. There is no better cure-all than ice cream or a Popsicle, or ultimately, a father's love.

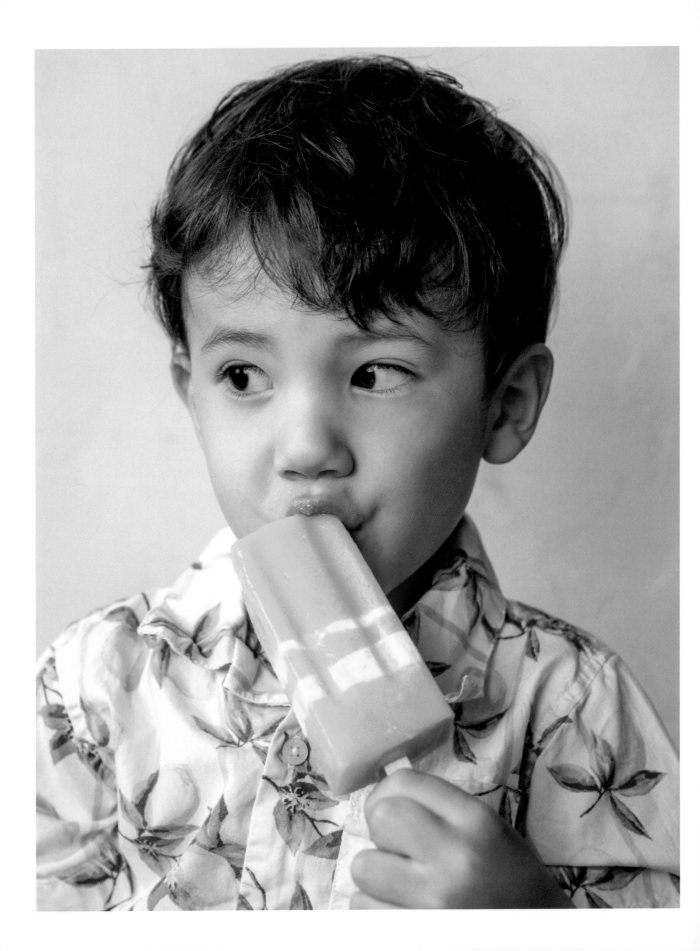

MAKES 6 TO 8 ICE POPS

INGREDIENTS

600 grams	1 pound 5 ounces	fresh pineapple cubes
600 grams	1 pound 5 ounces	fresh mango cubes
100 grams	½ cup	sugar*

* Depending on how ripe your fruits are, the level of sugar may vary. If your fruits are very ripe and sweet, you may not need any sugar at all.

Yogurt Layer (optional)

200 grams	¾ cup + 1 tablespoon	plain Greek yogurt* (preferably full-fat)
40 grams	¼ cup minus 2½ teaspoons	sugar
2 grams	½ teaspoon	vanilla extract

* You can also use your favorite flavor of yogurt.

EQUIPMENT

Blender	3- or 4-ounce (90 to 120 mL) ice pop molds
Small bowl	Ice pop sticks

1. In a blender, combine the pineapple and mango and blitz until smooth. Taste and add sugar as needed.

2. If making the yogurt layer: In a small bowl, stir together the yogurt, sugar, and vanilla.

3. Pour or spoon the mixture into 3- to 4-ounce (90 to 120 mL) ice pop molds. If using the yogurt, alternate the filling between the fruit and yogurt. Add ice pop sticks if they aren't already attached to the lids. Freeze for at least 6 to 8 hours or overnight.

4. To unmold, dip or run the molds under warm water to loosen and then slide them out. Serve immediately.

STORAGE

Best enjoyed immediately. To store, place in an airtight container in the freezer for up to 4 weeks.

JAZZ

POUND CAKE

ANNABELLE ALWAYS ATE with her eyes closed. One day, I had to ask: "Does it make the food taste better?"

Annabelle was a jazz pianist who frequented the bakery, and she explained that the inspiration for her melodies often comes from the flavors she's tasted in food. "I close my eyes to hear the notes," she explained. The higher trills are like dustings of sugar, the silky melodies smooth like butter and cream. Once in a while, there's a tart accent of acidity. "Pastries," she said, "sound just as sweet as they taste."

I had never thought of pastries through the lens of jazz before. Our kitchens function on carefully and scientifically measured recipes that leave little room for improvisation. But I do remember one of my side jobs when I was just starting out was at a place that only featured pound cakes. There was one base recipe that was so foolproof and resilient that it could be adapted into a variety of different cakes. Adding in chocolate took it in one direction; folding in dried fruits another. There was even a savory version with bacon and Gruyère.

"You have to absolutely learn the foundations of music first before you can be free to 'jazz it up,'" said Annabelle. "Several hundred chords and scales. But when you have the right foundations, you can begin to push the boundaries."

I think about that when I bake this pound cake recipe. How with a solid base of ingredients that are stable, there can be a little jazz in the pastry kitchen. Feel free to use this recipe as a starting point and make your own tune.

MAKES ONE 8½ × 4½-INCH (21.5 × 11.5 CM) LOAF (SERVES 6 TO 8)

INGREDIENTS

Softened unsalted butter and all-purpose flour, for the pan

295 grams	1⅓ cups + 3 tablespoons	sugar
211 grams	4 large	eggs
242 grams	1¾ cups	all-purpose flour
7 grams	1 tablespoon	baking powder
1 gram	¼ teaspoon	salt
126 grams	½ cup	heavy cream
7 grams	3½ teaspoons	lemon zest (from 1 lemon)
84 grams	6 tablespoons	unsalted butter, melted
26 grams	2 tablespoons + 1 teaspoon	rum (optional)

EQUIPMENT

8½ × 4½-inch (21.5 × 11.5 cm) loaf pan	Whisk
Mixing bowls	

1. Preheat the oven to 340°F (170°C).

2. Butter and flour the loaf pan: Butter the bottom, sides, and edges of an 8½ × 4½-inch (21.5 × 11.5 cm) loaf pan. Pour in a handful of flour and shake it around until the pan is evenly coated, then tap out any excess.

3. Make the batter: In a large mixing bowl, combine the sugar and eggs with a whisk until smooth and lightened in color.

4. In a separate bowl, whisk together the flour, baking powder, and salt until combined. Gradually add the dry ingredients to the sugar and egg mixture in batches, making sure one is fully incorporated before adding the next.

5. Pour in the cream and the lemon zest, stirring until combined. Add the melted butter and rum (if using) and stir until just combined.

6. Pour the batter into the pan (make sure not to fill it more than three-quarters of the way up, as the cake will rise in the oven).

7. Bake the cake: Bake until golden blond and a cake tester or paring knife inserted in the center comes out clean, 50 to 60 minutes.

8. Let the cake cool in the pan for 20 to 25 minutes. Run a paring knife around the edges of the cake. Unmold, slice, and serve.

STORAGE

Best enjoyed the day of baking. To store, wrap tightly in plastic wrap or place in an airtight container and keep at room temperature in a cool place for up to 2 days. You can also freeze the cake, wrapped tightly in plastic wrap and placed in an airtight container, for up to 3 weeks. To use the frozen loaf, remove from the container and transfer to the fridge (still in the plastic wrap) to thaw for at least 3 hours or overnight, until the cake has softened again.

BANOFFEE PIE

THERE ARE FEW better mentors I can imagine for a chef than Chef Daniel Boulud. I call him my "American Papa," and I will always remember my excitement when he invited me over to New York from France when I was twenty-eight years old. I worked in the kitchens of his restaurant Daniel, on the Upper East Side, for six years and was there when we won our third Michelin star.

Every time Daniel came through the doors of the kitchen from the dining room, our level of stress would rise. There was always something to fix, something to improve on, all while plating up the orders from the tickets quickly lining up at the stations. How I pushed back and fought Daniel during those first few years as a young kid from France!

But funny enough, while I learned to toughen up with my other bosses, with Daniel I learned the opposite. I learned that flexibility and open-mindedness are the most important skills of a leader. At Daniel, special requests, substitutions, and last-minute changes were something to expect daily. Learning to handle those changes to the daily rhythm makes a chef go from good to great. Daniel taught me it is much easier to say no than to take the effort to make yes happen.

In fact, the only thing I remember Daniel repeatedly saying no to was bananas and white chocolate. Both ingredients were strictly avoided on the dessert menu. You see, Daniel hated them. If you ever serve him either, watch as he discreetly pushes it aside with his fork and never touches it again.

These days, whenever someone asks me what I would create for Daniel if I wanted to make a dessert dedicated to him, I always answer the same thing: something with banana and white chocolate. I imagine caramelizing the bananas with rum and a dash of passion fruit to deglaze it and give it a floral hint. I would use the white chocolate to make a creamy ganache and the sweetness from the chocolate would replace the sugar.

It would be my biggest challenge, but those are the ones he's always taught me to take.

INGREDIENTS

Caramelized White Chocolate Diplomat Cream

282 grams	½ recipe	Pastry Cream (page 127), chilled for a few hours or overnight
263 grams	2 cups	chopped white chocolate
9 grams	1 tablespoon	fish gelatin powder
34 grams	2 tablespoons	water
150 grams	⅔ cup	heavy cream #1
263 grams	1 cup + 2 tablespoons	heavy cream #2

Caramelized Bananas

100 grams	½ cup	sugar
4 or 5 bananas, halved lengthwise		
15 grams	1 tablespoon	unsalted butter
60 grams	¼ cup	passion fruit puree or juice

Sablé Breton Cookie Base

57 grams	3 large	egg yolks
113 grams	½ cup	sugar
109 grams	1 stick (4 oz)	unsalted butter, very soft
152 grams	1 cup + 2 tablespoons	all-purpose flour
9 grams	2¼ teaspoons + ⅛ teaspoon	baking powder
1 gram	¼ teaspoon	Maldon sea salt
All-purpose flour, for dusting		

Assembly and Serving

58 grams	4 tablespoons (2 oz)	unsalted butter, melted
3 grams	¾ teaspoon	Maldon sea salt
Whipped cream		

EQUIPMENT

Sheet pan	Large saucepan or skillet
Silicone baking mat	9-inch (23 cm) glass or ceramic pie dish
Silicone and rubber spatulas	Baking sheet
Mixing bowls	Parchment paper (optional)
Whisk	Rolling pin
Immersion blender	Food processor
Stand mixer (or hand mixer)	

MAKE THE CARAMELIZED WHITE CHOCOLATE DIPLOMAT CREAM

1. Make the full recipe of pastry cream and chill as directed.

2. Preheat the oven to 265°F (130°C).

3. Caramelize the white chocolate: Line a sheet pan with a silicone baking mat (this will NOT work with parchment paper). Spread the chopped white chocolate evenly on the mat.

4. Bake until the chocolate caramelizes (it'll look like a thick paste and be light brown in color), about 45 minutes, using a silicone spatula to stir the chocolate around every 7 to 8 minutes.

5. Meanwhile, add the gelatin to the pastry cream: Remove the chilled pastry cream from the fridge and place in a large bowl. Use a rubber spatula to spread the pastry cream around the bowl so it becomes soft and spreadable.

6. In a small microwave-safe bowl, whisk the gelatin and water together until dissolved. Let sit for a few minutes until it's set. Microwave the mixture for 15 to 20 seconds, until it becomes a warm liquid, then pour it into the pastry cream. Fold with a spatula until combined.

7. Blend the chocolate: Scrape the caramelized white chocolate into a bowl. Pour in heavy cream #1 (⅔ cup/150 g) and use an immersion blender to blend until smooth. Pour the caramelized white chocolate mixture into the pastry cream mixture. Fold with a spatula until combined.

recipe continues

8. Whip the cream: In a stand mixer fitted with the whisk (or in a large bowl with a hand mixer or whisk), whip heavy cream #2 (1 cup + 2 tablespoons/263 g) on high speed until soft peaks form.

9. Fold the whipped cream into the pastry cream a little at a time with a rubber spatula, until just combined. Cover with plastic wrap pressed against the surface to prevent a skin from forming, and chill in the fridge until ready to assemble the pie.

MAKE THE CARAMELIZED BANANAS

10. Make a dry caramel: Place a large saucepan or skillet over medium heat. When the pan is hot, sprinkle the sugar in an even layer over the bottom of the pan. Cook, stirring with a wooden spoon or silicone spatula, until the sugar is blond in color, 1 to 2 minutes.

11. Caramelize the bananas: Place the bananas in the pan on top of the caramel in one even layer. Cook for 1 minute, then flip and cook for 1 minute more, until the bananas are soft but not overly mushy. Add the butter and the passion fruit puree/juice to deglaze the pan,* gently swirling the pan and turning the bananas to evenly coat them in the caramel. Remove from the heat.

> *Don't be intimidated—this isn't deglazing with alcohol like on TV, so you won't see a big flambé flame in your kitchen. Here, you're simply using a bit of liquid—in this case, the passion fruit purée and the moisture in the butter—to help lift the caramelized bananas from the bottom of the pan and prevent them from burning.*

12. Arrange the sliced bananas in the bottom of a 9-inch (23 cm) glass or ceramic pie dish in a circular pattern. Chill in the fridge until fully cooled.

MAKE THE SABLÉ BRETON COOKIE BASE

13. Combine the egg yolks and sugar: In a stand mixer fitted with the whisk (or with a hand mixer), combine the egg yolks and sugar and whip on high speed until light and fluffy, 2 to 3 minutes. Add the softened butter and whip until fully incorporated.

14. Add the dry ingredients: Add the flour, baking powder, and sea salt to the bowl and gently fold with a spatula until just combined.

15. Chill the dough: Turn the dough out onto a large piece of plastic wrap and gently form it into a ball. Wrap the dough in the plastic wrap. Flatten into a disc (it'll chill faster this way) and refrigerate until firm, 1 to 2 hours.

16. Preheat the oven to 350°F (175°C). Line a baking sheet with a silicone baking mat or parchment paper.

17. Shape the dough: Dust a work surface with flour. Roll out the dough to a rectangle about ½ inch (1.3 cm) thick. Transfer the dough to the prepared baking sheet. It doesn't really matter the shape or size of the dough, as you will be crumbling it up after it's baked.

18. Bake the cookie base: Bake the sablé Breton until golden brown, 20 to 25 minutes. The dough will puff up slightly in the oven because of the baking powder in it—that's okay, you want that light and airy texture. After removing from the oven, let it fully cool and then set aside until ready to assemble the pie.

ASSEMBLE THE PIE

19. Make the cookie crumbles: Use your hands or a food processor to break up the cooled cookie base into small crumbs and place the crumbs in a large bowl. Pour in the melted butter and sea salt and mix with a rubber spatula until evenly combined. You shouldn't be able to see individual crumbs once the crust is made.

20. Layer in the fillings: Remove the chilled pie pan from the fridge (the bananas should be fully cooled at this point). Spread a layer of the caramelized white chocolate diplomat over the bananas to fill the pan just below the top. Sprinkle the buttery cookie crumble mixture generously on top of the diplomat and gently press down with a flat-bottomed glass or measuring cup to form an even and tightly packed crust. Chill in the fridge for at least 1 hour before serving.

21. To serve: Carefully invert the pie onto a platter (so the bananas are now at the top). Hold it gently an inch or so above the platter so it wiggles itself out and onto the platter easily. Slice and serve with a dollop of fresh whipped cream.

STORAGE

Best enjoyed immediately. To store, cover with plastic wrap and keep in the refrigerator for 1 to 2 days.

PEACHES & SAUTERNES

WINSTON CHURCHILL ONCE SAID: "I am a man of simple tastes. I am easily satisfied with the best."

I laughed when I first read the quote because I agree with it completely. Some of the best meals in my life have been the easiest to prepare, and perfect in their own way.

One summer during my childhood, while I was begging for ice cream, my aunt offered me an alternative. She plucked a blood peach from our garden. While it was still warm from the sun, she sprinkled sugar on top and poured on a liberal amount of the red wine she was drinking, mixed it up, and gave it to me. It was France, it was the '80s—yes, she gave me a bit of wine. To this day, I remember the slight tanginess of the red wine and tannins. The ripe fruit segments almost melted on my tongue as if cooked down. And every bite released juicy sweetness that satisfied my dessert craving.

It took less than five minutes to make, and yet the flavors and experience lingered for a lifetime. The only caveat is that it isn't a recipe you can make at will. You are at the mercy of the right fruits and season. So when the summer peaches and stone fruits start appearing in your nearby farmers' markets, make sure you look for the ripest batch. A sweet dash of Sauternes—now my recommended wine of choice—some sugar, and a scoop of ice will make for glorious perfection.

SERVES 10

INGREDIENTS

	10	ripe peaches
350 grams	1½ cups	Sauternes
350 grams	1½ cups	water
	6 whole	star anise
70 grams	⅓ cup	sugar*

Whipped cream or crème fraîche, for serving

Ice cubes (optional)

> *The amount of sugar used will vary, depending on the sweetness of your Sauternes (some are much sweeter than others) and the ripeness of your peaches.*

---

recipe continues

EQUIPMENT

Large pot	Slotted spoon
Large bowl	Medium pot
Paring knife	Whisk

1. Blanch the peaches: Bring a large pot of water to a boil. Turn the heat down to medium. Make an ice bath by filling a large bowl with ice water, so once the peaches are blanched, you can cool them down right away.

2. Use a small paring knife to score an X into the bottom of each peach. Working in batches, carefully lower the peaches into the boiling water with a slotted spoon, making sure they are fully submerged. Blanch for 30 to 40 seconds (if your peaches are a bit less ripe, keep them in the hot water just a bit longer, so the peels loosen more).

3. Use the slotted spoon to transfer the peaches to the ice bath to "shock" them and stop the cooking process. Let the peaches cool for about 1 minute.

4. Peel and pit the peaches: Beginning at the bottoms where the Xs were scored, peel the skins away from the peach using your fingers or a paring knife. Slice the peaches in half and remove the pits.

5. Make the Sauternes syrup: In a medium pot, combine the Sauternes, water, star anise, and sugar and bring to a boil, whisking occasionally. Once boiling, turn the heat to the lowest setting.

6. Poach the peaches: Using a slotted spoon, carefully place the peach halves in the syrup, cover the pot, and let simmer until the peaches are tender and they can be easily pierced with a small paring knife (the time will depend on how ripe the peaches are; you'll want them to be tender but not so soft that they're mushy or fall apart). Remove from the heat and let fully chill in the fridge, a few hours.

7. To serve: Place 2 peach halves in each shallow serving bowl. Ladle or spoon a generous amount of the Sauternes syrup over the top. Serve with a dollop of whipped cream or crème fraîche. (Optional: This dish always reminds me of summertime and is meant to be served cold, so I like to add a few ice cubes to the bowl just before serving.)

STORAGE

Best enjoyed fresh the day of making. To store, cover loosely with plastic wrap or place in an airtight container and keep in the refrigerator for up to 2 days.

BRÛLÉED BROWN BUTTER MOCHI

IN 2013, MY wife and I took a small trip to Hawaii for five days. We called it our "last vacation." It was our first time away from the bakery since we opened. Little did we know, we'd come back home to the launch of the Cronut® and perhaps the toughest decade of our lives so far. Needless to say, we had no time off or any vacations during the years that followed. Every summer when the vast majority of the world traveled, we worked. And we were constantly getting catering requests for pastries for outdoor parties. The only problem is, very few pastries survive the heat and humidity of a New York summer.

"I wish we were back in Hawaii," I remember saying. Then, a lightbulb moment. If there was a place that knew how to make food to survive the sun, it would be Hawaii. And one of the desserts of choice there is the butter mochi.

Using a box of mochiko (sweet/glutinous rice flour) from our local Japanese convenience store, I made up a batch of brown butter mochi late at night in my home kitchen. Fragrant and nutty, it was chewy and slightly molten with a crispy crust. It starts with the essential ingredient, brown butter—butter that is simply melted down until it turns brown. You'll see its color change and darken. To add a special French touch, I brûléed the top by caramelizing sugar with a kitchen torch. It became my go-to for any outdoor event.

I could not think of a better source of inspiration than a place where "hello" and "good-bye" and "love" are all the same word. And where all the treats are filled with *aloha* spirit.

MAKES 12 PIECES

INGREDIENTS

115 grams	1 stick (4 oz)	unsalted butter, at room temperature
805 grams	Two 13.5-ounce cans	coconut milk
453 grams	1-pound box	mochiko flour (aka sweet/glutinous rice flour)
402 grams	2 cups	sugar
201 grams	4 large	eggs
12 grams	2¼ teaspoons	salt
8 grams	2 teaspoons	baking powder
4 grams	¾ teaspoon	vanilla paste or extract

Unsalted butter, for the baking dish

Granulated sugar, for brûléeing

EQUIPMENT

Small saucepan	Whisk
Silicone spatula	9 × 13-inch (23 × 33 cm) baking dish
Large heatproof bowl	Small handheld kitchen torch

1. Position a rack in the center of the oven and preheat the oven to 350°F (175°C).

2. **Make the brown butter:** In a small saucepan,* melt the butter over medium heat, stirring occasionally with a silicone spatula and swirling around the pan to help the butter melt evenly. After 4 to 5 minutes, the butter will start to foam. Continue cooking for a few more minutes, until it turns light golden brown and there's a nutty, lightly toasted aroma. Remove from the heat and transfer to a large heatproof bowl (so the butter doesn't continue to cook or burn).

   Use a light-colored pot when browning butter so you can easily watch the coloring. It's harder to tell in a darker pan, and the butter may overbrown and burn.

3. Make the batter: Add the coconut milk to the brown butter in the bowl, whisking gently until combined. Add the mochiko flour, sugar, eggs, salt, baking powder, and vanilla and whisk until smooth and there are no lumps.

4. Butter a 9 × 13-inch (23 × 33 cm) baking dish. Pour in the batter.

5. Bake until the top is golden brown, 1 hour to 1 hour 10 minutes.

6. Remove from the oven and let cool completely in the pan, about 1 hour (because mochi is very sticky, it's more difficult to slice when warm).

7. Slice and brûlé: Slice into 12 squares. Sprinkle a thin, even layer of granulated sugar across the top of each mochi square (enough so that you no longer see the surface of the mochi). Carefully and evenly brûlé the surface with a kitchen torch held about 4 inches from the surface* until golden caramel in color. Sprinkle more sugar and brûlé a second time as needed to create that golden caramelized crust.

Make sure to continuously move the torch across the mochi, so you don't brûlé one spot for too long. Remember, even when you've stopped torching, the sugar is still extremely hot and will continue to caramelize, and you don't want it to burn.

8. Let stand for 5 minutes, until the sugar fully cools and hardens, then enjoy.

STORAGE

Best enjoyed immediately. To store, cover with plastic wrap or place in an airtight container and keep at room temperature for up to 2 days.

CHAPTER 5
The Traditions

The things we love so much, we do over and over again. These become our tried-and-true recipes for holidays, birthdays, and showstopping moments.

BABA AU RHUM IN A JAR

SO MUCH OF the magic and hard work for a dinner party takes place prior to the event itself. And no one is a better party planner in my mind than Martha Stewart. The first time I visited Martha's house in Bedford, New York, I was working at Restaurant Daniel and was catering desserts for a dinner event for her. It was meant to be an "intimate party for twenty," but as I pulled up to the property, it seemed like a full-scale production was in place: florists were loading in beautifully decorated centerpieces, tableware was being brought out and polished. And yet despite the busy energy and flow of people, every little bit of the dining room and kitchen was clean and organized. It looked like a stage version of a perfect home.

Like the conductor of an orchestra, Martha was at the center of it all. I remember even in the chaos of everything, she looked up and smiled at me. Martha is a wealth of knowledge, and if you ever spend five minutes with her, she'll probably teach you something you never knew before. She waved me over to her kitchen table and showed me how she would be doing an episode about salads in mason jars soon for her show. I loved the idea of how she put the ingredients in the jar, built her salad for later, and had it individually portioned.

A few years later, I remembered Martha's mason jars and decided to put them to use my way. One of my favorite things to make is baba au rhum—a soft brioche-like cake that is soaked thoroughly in rum syrup and topped with a dollop of whipped cream. Boozy and melt-in-your-mouth tender, it makes for the perfect end to a dinner party. And it is the perfect choice to make the day before so that it can thoroughly soak. I use individual mason jars to hold the baba with its delicious rum syrup, and when it comes time for dessert, I simply bring the jars out onto the table. It's become a go-to recipe for dinner parties, letting me work ahead, saving me time and hassle.

And as Martha would say, "Life is too complicated not to be orderly."

MAKES 6 SERVINGS

INGREDIENTS

Babas

30 grams	3½ tablespoons	active dry yeast
60 grams	¼ cup	water
228 grams	1½ cups + 1 tablespoon	bread flour
45 grams	3 tablespoons + 2 teaspoons	sugar
142 grams	3 large	eggs
103 grams	7 tablespoons + ¾ teaspoon (4 oz)	unsalted butter, at room temperature
3 grams	⅔ teaspoon	sea salt

Softened butter, for the baba molds

Rum Syrup

995 grams	4 cups + 2 tablespoons	water
360 grams	1¾ cups	sugar

Vanilla seeds (scraped from 3 vanilla beans) or 1½ teaspoons vanilla extract

10 grams	5 teaspoons	grated lemon zest (from 1½ lemons)
10 grams	5 teaspoons	grated orange zest (from 1 orange)
45 grams	¼ cup	passion fruit puree (1½ whole fruits)
60 grams	¼ cup	rum

Vanilla Whipped Cream

200 grams	¾ cup + 2½ teaspoons	heavy cream
20 grams	1 tablespoon + ¾ teaspoon	sugar

Vanilla seeds (scraped from 1 vanilla bean) or ½ teaspoon vanilla extract

EQUIPMENT

Small bowl

Stand mixer with a dough hook

Piping bag

6 stainless steel or nonstick metal baba molds (2½ inches/6.5 cm) deep

Medium pot

Six 16-ounce glass mason jars

MAKE THE BABAS (DAY BEFORE)

1. In a small bowl, stir together the yeast and water until dissolved.

2. Mix the dough: In a stand mixer fitted with the dough hook, combine the yeast mixture with the flour, sugar, and eggs. Mix on medium speed until all the items are incorporated. Turn the mixer to high speed and mix until the dough develops elasticity and springs back quickly when pulled.

3. Add the butter and sea salt and continue mixing on high until fully incorporated. The final texture will be stretchy and elastic when you pull it.

4. Fill the molds: Fill a piping bag with the dough. Grease 6 stainless steel or nonstick metal baba molds (2½ inches/6.5 cm deep) with softened butter (make sure to get into the base edges). Fill each mold with 90 grams of dough.*

  * The dough is very soft and loose, so you can use kitchen scissors to cut the ribbon of dough as it's piped out.

5. Let the dough rise: Set the baba molds in a humid and warm place to proof until the dough doubles in volume, 15 to 25 minutes (it may take longer, depending on the temperature of your space).

6. Preheat the oven to 340°F (170°C).

7. Bake the babas: Bake until golden brown and the dough springs back to the touch, 25 to 35 minutes.

recipe continues

8. Let the babas cool in the molds for 5 minutes, then unmold them while they're still hot. (They need to be warm when you add the rum syrup.)

MEANWHILE, MAKE THE RUM SYRUP

9. In a medium pot, bring the water and sugar to a boil over high heat, whisking occasionally until all the sugar has dissolved. Remove from the heat.

10. Add the vanilla seeds (or extract), lemon zest, and orange zest and let it infuse in the hot syrup for 15 minutes.

11. Add the passion fruit puree and rum. Set aside and let cool for 15 to 20 minutes before soaking the baba.

12. Soak the baba: Make sure the baba and the syrup are both warm (a bit hotter than body temperature).* Dunk the baba in the syrup, gently pressing each baba to let the air out and the syrup in. It will feel like pressing a sponge under water. Let the baba sit in the syrup for a few minutes.

   * *With soaking, temperature is everything. Having the baba and syrup the same warm temperature allows the liquid to absorb more thoroughly.*

13. Repeat the soaking and pressing process one to two more times if needed so the babas are fully soaked. When fully soaked, the babas should feel heavier and the syrup will come out when gently pressed. (I like to add an extra splash of rum right after they're fully soaked.) Place each baba into a mason jar and fill the jars with the soaking liquid.

14. Chill the soaked babas: Transfer the soaked babas in the mason jars to the refrigerator and chill for 1 to 2 hours or up to overnight.

MAKE THE VANILLA WHIPPED CREAM

15. In a stand mixer fitted with the whisk (or in a large glass bowl with a whisk), mix together the heavy cream, sugar, and vanilla seeds (or extract).

recipe continues

16. Whip on high speed until soft peaks form, just a few minutes.

17. To serve: Place each baba on its side on a plate or in a shallow bowl. Slice the baba open lengthwise. Spoon some of the soaking liquid over the top and into the bowl.

18. Add a generous dollop of vanilla whipped cream over the baba. Enjoy! (Traditionally, we pour a bit of additional rum over the top, too, but this is optional.)

STORAGE

Best enjoyed right away. Soaked babas can be kept in the mason jars in the refrigerator (separate from the syrup) for 1 to 2 days.

BUTTERMILK PANCAKES

IN MY FAMILY, we celebrate with pancakes. We decided there's something special about kickstarting any celebration the moment you wake up. Why wait until after dinner to have your cake? Whether you're celebrating a piece of good news, a birthday, a homecoming, or something as simple as a Sunday—pancakes hit the spot. That way the first bite of your day can be your sweetest. The day that I found out I was having a son, my wife had started off the morning making pancakes. Immediately, I asked her what we were celebrating. It wasn't until I saw a miniature pancake stack next to mine that I realized the news.

Just like eggs can be done according to an individual's preferences, pancakes also come in a wide range of variations. There are thinner ones, thicker ones, fluffy soufflé ones stacked in a jiggly tower. The ones I make for my family at home are from a modified cake recipe. They come out fluffy and soft and moderately tall. A good pan liberally covered with melted butter (not sprayed with oil) makes the edges crisp up and brown. And once the batter hits the pan, you turn down the fire so that the pancake slowly simmers before being flipped over. For some, pancakes may be seen as a rather casual item, commonly made for no special occasion at all. But for me, a pancake is a luxury. It says that there's a little extra time in the morning today to make something from scratch.

Whenever I wake up to the smell of pancakes, I know it's a day of celebration. It's a little secret language where the smell of syrup and browning butter instantly makes me happier. And usually the taller the stack, the better the news.

MAKES 8 TO 10 PANCAKES

INGREDIENTS

10 grams	2¼ teaspoons	baking soda
18 grams	4 teaspoons	baking powder
18 grams	4¼ teaspoons + a pinch	sugar
6 grams	1 teaspoon	salt
310 grams	2¾ cups	pastry flour
45 grams	1 large	egg
530 grams	2¼ cups	buttermilk
63 grams	4½ tablespoons	unsalted butter, melted

Butter for cooking

Maple syrup and your favorite toppings, for serving

EQUIPMENT

Large bowl	Ladle
Whisk	Offset spatula or pancake turner
Nonstick skillet	

1. In a large bowl, combine the baking soda, baking powder, sugar, salt, and flour with a whisk. Stir in the egg, then add the buttermilk and melted butter until evenly combined.

2. In a nonstick skillet, melt a tablespoon of butter over medium-low heat. Ladle ½ cup of batter into the pan, then cook for 2 to 3 minutes (the center will start to bubble). Flip and cook until the other side is golden brown, 1 to 2 minutes more. Continue until you've used all the batter, adding about ½ tablespoon of butter to the pan between each pancake.

3. Enjoy with maple syrup and your favorite toppings.

STORAGE

Best enjoyed immediately.

VANILLA BLANC-MANGER

WHEN WE FIRST met Sara, a regular guest at the bakery, she was sketching a picture of one of our pastries on a small piece of card stock. The cake that sat in front of her cast a shadow on the marble tabletop and almost looked like a model posing for a photograph. Besides her day job, Sara was an illustrator, and her specialty was making greeting cards inspired by the different delights she found in everyday life in New York, including those that come in the form of sugar and spice.

She called them "no occasion cards" because they were blank inside, and because Sara believed there needn't ever be a reason required for sending someone a kind note. "Just because," she said, while using a small ballpoint pen to add in the details of the raspberry pavlova she was sketching.

One day she happily announced that she'd be taking a stab not just at drawing pastries but baking them herself. When I asked for what occasion, she explained that, just like with her cards, none was needed. Sara's favorite dessert was a *blanc-manger*, a classic French milk pudding that literally means "white eating." Ethereal, silky, and subtle—it is one of the desserts that satisfies without ever being decadent. "Effortless," she said.

It wasn't until years later that I realized how fitting it was for Sara that her favorite dessert is "blanc" or "blank," like the inside of her greeting cards. And that it requires no occasion at all to enjoy. And in fact, it's a chilled dessert that requires no baking at all either.

SERVES 5 OR 6

INGREDIENTS

5 grams	2 teaspoons	unflavored gelatin powder
65 grams	¼ cup	water
400 grams	1¾ cups	heavy cream
100 grams	⅓ cup	condensed milk

Vanilla seeds (scraped from 1 vanilla bean) or ½ teaspoon vanilla extract

recipe continues

EQUIPMENT

Small bowl	5 or 6 ceramic ramekins, about 3½ inches (9 cm) in diameter and 2 inches (5 cm) deep
Whisk	
Medium pot	Small offset spatula

1. In a small bowl, whisk together the gelatin and water and let sit for a few minutes to bloom (the gelatin has absorbed the majority of the liquid, gaining 2 to 3 times its original volume, and feels firm and set).

2. In a medium pot, bring the cream, condensed milk, and vanilla seeds (or extract) to a simmer over medium heat, stirring constantly with a whisk (do not boil). (Because the condensed milk contains sugar, watch this carefully and make sure the bottom doesn't burn.) Remove from the heat.

3. Stir the gelatin mixture into the milk mixture until dissolved and evenly combined.

4. Divide the custard among 5 or 6 ceramic ramekins, about 3½ inches (9 cm) in diameter and 2 inches (5 cm) deep, filling until just about full.

5. Chill in the fridge until set (when the custard is no longer a liquid and the texture is slightly wobbly when jiggled), a few hours.

6. To serve, run a small offset spatula around the edges of a ramekin to gently loosen the blanc-manger. Place a plate over the ramekin and carefully invert to unmold. Serve immediately.

STORAGE

Best enjoyed right away. Blanc-manger still in their ramekins can be covered with plastic wrap pressed against the surface to prevent a skin from forming and kept in the refrigerator for up to 2 days. (Once unmolded, they will start to lose their shape, so if you plan on storing, keep them in their molds.)

SNOW-COVERED BEIGNETS

DURING THE HOLIDAYS, the kitchen is the warmest place in our house. The oven is always preheated, ready to bake off something hearty. The stovetop is tightly packed with pots and pans, each carrying an entrée, appetizer, or snack. We huddle inside while the first few snowflakes start to drift down outside. I always love how after that first big snowstorm we wake up to powdery stacks of snow that sit on top of our backyard garden tables and look like white cakes.

Then one year we received an email asking for some suggestions for treats to bake at home to celebrate a group that was the proud winner of their town's annual snowman competition. The categories ranged from "most traditional" to "funniest" to "most unexpected." The photos of the snowmen that followed brought a smile to my face—the theme they chose was yoga, and their snowmen were doing different yoga poses. I loved the idea that snow is such a moldable medium it can become anything we shape it into.

Instantly the thought of a beignet recipe popped into my head. There's something about pillowy beignets, lightly crisp on the outside and filled with steam within. And with, of course, the final touch of liberally dusting a mountain of powdered sugar on top of them, like snow falling onto our tables, ready to become white cakes or snowmen or anything your heart desires.

MAKES 15 TO 20 BEIGNETS

INGREDIENTS

1 kilogram	1 recipe	Brioche Dough (page 34)
All-purpose flour, for dusting		
Grapeseed oil, for deep-frying		
200 grams	1 cup	powdered sugar
Crushed peppermint candies (optional)		

recipe continues

EQUIPMENT

Rolling pin

Sharp knife or pizza cutter

Wire rack

Baking sheet

Large pot

Digital/candy thermometer

Slotted spoon

Small sieve/sifter

1. Make the brioche dough (day before): Make the dough as directed through the second fermentation (step 7) and refrigerate overnight.

2. Shape and cut the dough: Remove the chilled dough from the fridge, unwrap it, and transfer to a heavily floured work surface. Using a rolling pin, roll out the dough into a rectangle that's about ½ inch (1.3 cm) thick.

3. Using a sharp knife or a pizza cutter, cut 2⅜-inch (6 cm) squares of dough. Lay the squares on a baking sheet and let sit out in a warm area slightly above room temperature for about 30 minutes to 1 hour, so they come to room temp and puff up just a bit.*

 *The squares of dough can be placed on a tray and wrapped tightly
  with plastic wrap and kept in the fridge for up to 24 hours.*

4. Fry the beignets: Place a wire cooling rack on a baking sheet (or line the baking sheet with paper towels). Fill a large pot with 2½ to 3 inches (6.5 to 7.5 cm) of oil and heat over medium heat until it reaches 355°F (180°C) on a digital/candy thermometer.

5. Using a slotted spoon, gently lower a few dough squares into the oil, working in batches as needed so your pot doesn't get overcrowded.* Fry on one side until puffed up and golden, 2 to 3 minutes. Flip them over to fry on the other side until golden brown. Remove from the oil and drain on the cooling rack or paper towels. Continue with the remaining dough squares.

 *Adding too many beignets in at once will lower the temperature
  of the oil and you won't get an even fry.*

6. Dust generously with lots of powdered sugar and crushed peppermint candies (if using), and enjoy while they're still warm.

VANILLA BEAN
BIRTHDAY CAKE WITH
HOMEMADE SPRINKLES

I'VE ALWAYS THOUGHT that sprinkles were something created in America. To my surprise, they were invented in France! Also called "nonpareils" (without parallel), they were later commercialized by the Dutch and used to top bread with butter. And here I was thinking they were only for cupcakes.

I've always loved the celebration of colors, but I don't like store-brought sprinkles because I don't know what ingredients went into them. Then one year, I met a food scientist who was studying the effects of color on appetite. He had been experimenting with eating all his foods on a blue plate to see if it was effective in suppressing his appetite. On the opposite end of the spectrum, yellows and oranges were said to increase appetite. And apparently green-colored foods may feel "healthier," whether or not they truly are.

For his next study, he was planning to test the perceived flavor differences in foods that were a color other than the one usually associated with them. Purple carrots instead of orange. Yellow watermelons instead of red. He explained to me that, ultimately, it was good to "eat the rainbow" as often as we can.

Inspired by his findings, I made my son a confetti cake for his birthday that year, filled with sprinkles that I had made myself and with colors that he had chosen. I mixed together powdered sugar and egg whites with a rainbow of natural colors—and even some gold dust—and cut out different shapes. I even added a bit of pumpkin seed oil to the cake so it had a green color. I asked him how the colors made him feel and whether they changed his appetite, curious as to whether the food scientist was right. My son looked at me and simply answered: happy.

MAKES AN 8-INCH (20 CM) SIX-LAYER CAKE (SERVES 6 TO 8)

INGREDIENTS

Sprinkles

500 grams	4 cups	powdered sugar
10 grams	2 teaspoons	lemon juice
60 grams	2 large	egg whites

Liquid food coloring (various colors)

Vanilla Chantilly

8 grams	2½ teaspoons + ⅛ teaspoon	unsweetened gelatin powder
50 grams	¼ cup	water
351 grams	1½ cups	heavy cream #1
116 grams	½ cup + 3¾ teaspoons	sugar

Vanilla seeds (scraped from 2 to 3 vanilla beans) or 1½ teaspoons vanilla extract

273 grams	1¼ cups	mascarpone
696 grams	3 cups	heavy cream #2

Almond Genoise Cake

Softened butter and all-purpose flour, for the cake pan

345 grams	7 large	eggs
345 grams	1¾ cups	sugar
272 grams	2¼ cups	all-purpose flour
11 grams	2⅛ teaspoons	baking powder
137 grams	1½ cups	almond flour
226 grams	1 cup	Greek yogurt (preferably full-fat)
64 grams	⅓ cup	pumpkin seed oil

EQUIPMENT

Baking sheet(s)

Parchment paper

Stencils with small cutouts, like small stars, circles, hearts, etc.

Piping bag with small plain tip (optional)

Stand mixer (or hand mixer)

Mixing bowls

Offset spatula

Whisk

Medium pot

Immersion blender

Two 8-inch (20 cm) round cake pans

Rubber spatula

Large serrated knife

Rotating cake stand (optional)

9- to 10-inch (23 to 25 cm) round cake board

MAKE THE SPRINKLES (2 DAYS BEFORE)

1. Line a baking sheet(s) with parchment paper (you may need a few baking sheets, depending on how many sprinkle colors and shapes you want to make). Lay stencils* with small cutouts, like small stars, circles, hearts, etc., on top.

  * *If you don't have stencils, you can also use a small piping bag fitted with a small plain tip, at least ⅛ inch (½ cm). See step 4 for more detail.*

2. Make the icing: In a stand mixer fitted with the whisk (or with a hand mixer), combine the powdered sugar, lemon juice, and egg whites and mix until light and fluffy. If the mixture feels a bit dry, add a few drops of water as needed to make a smooth consistency.

3. Color the icing: Divide the mixture into mixing bowls, one bowl for each color/ shape of sprinkle you want to make. Stir in 1 or 2 drops of food coloring to your desired color.* Cover the bowls you're not immediately working with with plastic wrap so the icing doesn't dry out.

  * *A little food coloring goes a long way, so start with 1 or 2 drops at first, and add more as needed.*

recipe continues

4. Using an offset spatula, spread the icing across the stencils.* Gently lift off the stencils, then let the sprinkles fully dry and harden on the parchment (this may take up to 24 hours or more). Repeat with the remaining icing colors and designs.

> *If you don't have stencils, transfer the colored icing into a small piping bag fitted with a small plain tip. Pipe long lines of icing onto the parchment paper and let fully dry and harden. When ready to decorate your cake, break the icing into smaller sprinkles.*

5. Once hardened, carefully loosen the sprinkles from the parchment and store in an airtight container until ready to use.

MAKE THE VANILLA CHANTILLY (DAY BEFORE)

6. In a small bowl, whisk together the gelatin and water until dissolved. Let the mixture sit a few minutes until the gelatin has bloomed (when it has absorbed the majority of the liquid, gaining 2 to 3 times its original volume, and feels firm and set).

7. In a medium pot, combine the heavy cream #1 (1½ cups/ 351 g) and the sugar and bring to a simmer over medium heat, stirring occasionally with a whisk until the sugar is dissolved. Do not boil.

8. Stir in the gelatin mixture and vanilla seeds (or extract) until combined. Remove from the heat.

9. Place the mascarpone in a large bowl. Carefully pour the hot milk mixture over the mascarpone and use an immersion blender to blend until smooth.

10. Pour in the heavy cream #2 (3 cups/696 g) and blend until smooth. Cover in plastic wrap that touches the surface to prevent a skin from forming. Refrigerate until set (the texture should be very thick and jiggly, and no longer a liquid), a few hours or up to overnight.* Keep chilled until ready to serve.

> *This Chantilly recipe should be made the day before so it's fully set and chilled before frosting the cake.*

recipe continues

MAKE THE ALMOND GENOISE CAKE

11. Position a rack in the center of the oven and preheat the oven to 350°F (175°C). Butter two 8-inch (20 cm) round cake pans, coating the bottom and sides well. Pour a handful of flour into each pan and shake it around until the pans are evenly coated, then tap out any excess.

12. Make the batter: In a stand mixer fitted with the whisk (or in a large bowl with a hand mixer), combine the eggs and sugar. Mix on high speed until light and fluffy.

13. In a bowl, whisk together the all-purpose flour, baking powder, and almond flour until combined. While continuing to mix on high speed, add the dry ingredients to the egg mixture in three additions, making sure each addition is fully incorporated before adding the next. Do not overmix. Turn off the mixer.

14. Fold in the yogurt and pumpkin seed oil with a rubber spatula until fully combined.

15. Fill each prepared cake pan with batter so they're about 80 percent full (the cake will rise a bit in the oven).

16. Bake the cakes: Bake until golden brown and a cake tester inserted into the middle comes out clean, 17 to 20 minutes. Let cool for 15 minutes in the pan, then unmold onto a wire rack to let fully cool.

17. Slice each cake layer into thirds: Using a serrated knife, slice each (fully cooled) layer horizontally into thirds.* If your layers have domed during baking, don't worry—simply slice off the top dome so you're left with a flat surface (bonus: you can snack on the cake scraps while you frost the cake!). You'll end up with layers that are about ¾ inch (2 cm) thick.

> *To ensure even layers, place the cake on a rotating cake stand and use your serrated knife to gently score all the way around the sides of the cake to measure and mark off the thirds. Then gently saw along the score marks into the cake, holding the knife level, until you have three even flat layers.

18. Whip the vanilla Chantilly: Bring the chilled vanilla Chantilly out of the fridge (it should be very thick and fully set by this point: no longer a liquid and jiggly in texture). Use a stand mixer fitted with a whisk (or a hand mixer) to whip the chilled Chantilly* until fluffy medium peaks form, so it's smooth and spreadable.

  Make sure your Chantilly is cold. If it's room temperature
  or warm, it won't whip up into fluffy peaks.

19. Frost the cake: Place the first layer of cake onto a 9- to 10-inch (23 to 25 cm) round cake board. Using an offset spatula, scoop a dollop of Chantilly onto the center of the cake layer. Starting from the center and working your way outward, spread an even layer of Chantilly that's the same thickness as the cake layer. Repeat this process with the remaining cake layers.*

  A rotating cake stand helps with the frosting process
  here to ensure even layers and frosting.

20. Finish frosting and chill the cake: Place a larger dollop of frosting on the top layer, spread it outward and partly down the sides, adding more along the sides as needed until the cake is fully frosted and smooth. Chill the cake for at least 30 minutes before decorating with sprinkles and serving.

21. Decorate the cake: Decorate with assorted sprinkles, then slice and serve. When you're ready to slice, dip a sharp knife into a container of boiling water (or run it under very hot water for at least 30 seconds) to heat up the blade. This will give you neat and clean slices so you can see all those beautiful layers without the Chantilly smearing. Clean your knife and redip it into the hot water before each cut.

STORAGE

Best enjoyed immediately.

COCONUT ÎLE FLOTTANTE

HENRY'S RESUME LANDED in my inbox one morning. Thirty years at the Pentagon, and now he was thinking about becoming a baker. I was curious as to why he wanted to take such a dramatic turn so late in life and decided to offer him a short stint for a few months during the winter. So, every morning, Henry would show up to work early and start the daily production with the team. He found incredible joy in the repetition of tasks—peeling apples for pie, or matching macaron shells together to make sure they were uniform in size. After a few months of long hours on his feet, however, I could tell it was wearing him down.

"Baking one cake at home is certainly different from baking a hundred cakes," he said to me.

To which I responded, "Staying at a hotel in a tropical island is better than working for a hotel on a tropical island." A few weeks later, Henry purchased a ticket to visit Hawaii with his wife. While he had enjoyed the kitchen, it was not for him in the long term. As part of his retirement gift, we made him a special dessert.

In a bain-marie, we gently baked meringues until they were tender and then lightly placed them on top of warm crème anglaise. To go along with the theme of his vacation location, we added some coconut milk.

"Presenting the *île flottante*," I said, "which translates to 'floating island.'" I remember the smile on Henry's face when I told him that. Now he could "bake his cake and eat it too."

INGREDIENTS

Caramel Powder

300 grams	1½ cups	sugar

Coconut Crème Anglaise

100 grams	½ cup	milk
275 grams	1¼ cups	coconut milk
75 grams	¼ cup + ½ tablespoon	heavy cream
120 grams	6 large	egg yolks
75 grams	⅓ cup + 4 teaspoons	sugar

Meringue

350 grams	12 large	egg whites
175 grams	¾ cup + 2 tablespoons	sugar

Poaching Liquid

2 kilograms	½ gallon	whole milk

EQUIPMENT

Baking sheet	Silicone spatula
Silicone baking mat or parchment paper	Digital thermometer
Mixing bowls	Stand mixer
Medium saucepan	Large ladle
Food processor	Piping bag
Medium pot	Slotted spoon
Whisk	

MAKE THE COCONUT CRÈME ANGLAISE (DAY BEFORE)

1. Heat the milk mixture: In a medium pot, bring the milk, coconut milk, and cream to a boil over medium-high heat while stirring with a whisk. Remove from the heat.

2. In a bowl, whisk together the egg yolks and sugar until fully combined.

3. Temper the egg yolk mixture: While whisking, slowly pour one-third of the hot milk mixture into the egg yolk mixture and whisk until fully incorporated to temper the eggs. Whisk in another one-third of the milk mixture, then pour the tempered egg mixture back into the pot with the remaining milk mixture, stirring until combined.

4. Make the crème anglaise: Cook the custard over medium heat, stirring constantly with a silicone spatula, until it reaches 185°F (85°C) on a digital thermometer and it's thick enough to coat the back of the spatula, 4 to 5 minutes. (If you can swipe your finger through the custard on the back of the spatula and the line left by your finger remains, it's ready!). Remove from the heat and let fully cool in the fridge, a few hours or up to overnight.

MAKE THE CARAMEL POWDER

5. Make a dry caramel: Line a baking sheet with a silicone baking mat or parchment paper. Put the granulated sugar in a small bowl and set it near the stove. Place a medium saucepan over medium heat. When the pan is hot, sprinkle a thin, even layer of sugar over the bottom of the pan. As the sugar melts and caramelizes, slowly sprinkle in more sugar, one small handful at a time, gently stirring with a silicone spatula and making sure each handful has reached an amber brown color before adding another handful. Once all the sugar has been added, cook until it has turned golden amber brown, 1 to 2 minutes. Remove from the heat immediately to keep it from burning.*

   * *You can move the pan on and off the heat to control the temperature to make sure your sugar doesn't burn and instead stays a golden amber brown.*

6. Pour the caramel immediately onto the prepared baking sheet in one even layer. Let cool to room temperature, until hardened, 10 to 15 minutes. Using the back of a spoon, break the caramel into small pieces. Place the pieces into a food processor and blitz into a fine powder. Set aside.

recipe continues

MAKE THE MERINGUE

7. In a stand mixer fitted with the whisk, whip the egg whites on high speed until they're foamy, 1 to 2 minutes. Gradually add the sugar a little at a time while continuing to mix on high speed, until stiff peaks form.

POACH THE MERINGUE

8. Pour 5 inches (13 cm) milk into a medium pot. Bring the milk to a simmer over medium-low heat (do not boil).

9. Shape the meringues: Fill a bowl with water. Dip a ladle into the water to wet it (this allows the meringue to release from the ladle when poaching). Place a few large scoops of meringue into a piping bag and cut a large opening at the tip of the piping bag. Pipe enough meringue into the ladle to create a dome, and use your hands or a small spatula to create a clean smooth ball shape. Use your hands/spatula to clean off any excess meringue on the bottom of the ladle.

10. Add the meringue to the poaching liquid: While the milk is still simmering over medium-low heat, dunk the ladle into it all the way down to the bottom of the pot, making sure the meringue is fully submerged. Hold for a few seconds until the ball of meringue releases and pops up to the surface. Allow the meringue to poach for 2 minutes, then use a spatula or the ladle to gently flip the meringue and cook for another 2 minutes.

11. Using a slotted spoon, gently lift the meringue and transfer it to a baking sheet. Repeat this process with the remaining meringue.

12. To serve: Gently place a poached meringue into a bowl. Ladle a generous amount of the cooled coconut crème anglaise over the top. Sprinkle the meringue with a bit of caramel powder and serve.

STORAGE

Best enjoyed right away. The poached meringues can be kept on the baking sheet in the refrigerator for up to 1 day until ready to serve. The coconut crème anglaise can be kept in an airtight container in the refrigerator for 2 to 3 days.

FAMILY HEIRLOOMS
SABLÉS VIENNOIS

FOR MY IN-LAWS, cooking is part of family history. My wife has rice wine that was passed down from her great-grandmother as part of her ancestor's dowry in China. There's even a braising liquid that has been passed down multiple generations, acting like a rolling stock of flavor. And when my wife's grandparents passed away, the one thing of theirs she wished she had kept was the wok that her grandmother cooked most of their family dinners in. She swears that the flavors of food cooked in it are the only ones that taste exactly like her childhood.

I have always been envious of family heirlooms, as my family didn't keep many. Knowing that previous generations have experienced something similar brings so much more depth to each bite. Food no longer tastes "savory" or "tender"; it tastes "like home" or "like our childhood."

A few years ago, I decided I wanted to make a contribution to the family legacy by creating a new family heirloom. It was one of the first recipes I had learned in culinary school, and it was rumored to be one of the oldest recipes in France. Sablés Viennois, also called Danish butter cookies, are flaky and tender cookies that can be piped in a variety of shapes, from rosettes to waves to thin fingers. On the surface, they seem straightforward and relatively plain, but they become addictive, and soon you'll find you've eaten the whole batch.

This is the first cookie recipe I taught my mother-in-law, a notoriously picky eater. And now in the large family book of Chinese recipes, there's a little French contribution.

MAKES 20 TO 30 COOKIES

INGREDIENTS

145 grams	1 cup + 2½ teaspoons	powdered sugar
361 grams	3 sticks + 1½ tablespoons (11 oz)	unsalted butter, at room temperature
435 grams	3⅓ cups	all-purpose flour
1 gram	½ teaspoon	salt
57 grams	2 large	egg whites
1 gram	½ teaspoon	vanilla paste or extract

EQUIPMENT

Baking sheet	Rubber spatula
Silicone baking mat or parchment paper	Piping bag with star tip (Ateco 824)
Stand mixer (or hand mixer)	

1. Preheat the oven to 350°F (180°C). Line a baking sheet with a silicone baking mat or parchment paper.

2. In a stand mixer fitted with the paddle (or a hand mixer), cream together the powdered sugar and butter on high speed until light and fluffy. Add the flour, salt, egg whites, and vanilla. Continue mixing until evenly combined.

3. Using a rubber spatula, transfer the batter into a piping bag fitted with a star tip (Ateco 824). Pipe the batter onto the prepared baking sheet in round rosettes or swirls, each 2½ to 3 inches (6.5 to 7.5 cm) wide.

4. Bake until the cookies are lightly golden, 10 to 12 minutes depending on the size.

5. Let cool fully on the baking sheet, then enjoy.

STORAGE

To store, place in an airtight container and keep at room temperature in a cool place for up to 2 weeks.

CROQUEMBOUCHE

SOMEONE ONCE ASKED me to rank the pastries that are the hardest to make in the French repertoire. I thought long and hard because each has its own challenges. To be honest, perfecting any pastry is difficult. A soufflé could collapse, ice cream could crystallize, and even a simple crêpe could burn and stick to the pan. Finally, I decided that the one pastry item most patissiers would see as advanced would be: the croquembouche.

Translated literally as "crunch in your mouth," a croquembouche is a tower of cream puffs, each filled with light cream and dipped in caramel to form a hard shell. Imagine building a delicate house of cards, but with pastry. To properly construct the foundation, each little ball of choux dough needs to be equal in size and placed together at the perfect angle. Using hot caramel to seal the choux together, your hands have to work fast, and there's little room for error. And of course, you cannot build this a day in advance, as humidity will cause it to deteriorate and collapse.

In France, large competitions are held among professionals who use these same building blocks of little choux cream puffs and caramel to assemble large structures. A train, a monument, the Eiffel Tower. Back in Paris, I would build ten to twelve croquembouches every day at Fauchon, one of the top patisseries in Paris—the smallest being two to three feet tall and the largest being fifteen feet. We then pulled sugar flowers and ribbons to decorate each one. Altogether, it can take from several hours up to an entire day, even with multiple people working on it, to create one croquembouche.

One day, I was asked to teach a class of home cooks how to make a croquembouche. The class was called "Pastry Bucket List." The students showed up excited and nervous. But luckily everyone went home with an assembled tower of some sort and there were no catastrophes. After the class, one of the students approached me and asked if I had any tips or tricks. Did I think a ring was better than a cone? Maybe we could add some corn syrup to the caramel to keep it from crystallizing? I smiled and told him the only "trick" that is foolproof is practice. Just because something is on your bucket list, doesn't mean you will experience it only once in your lifetime.

MAKES 1 CROQUEMBOUCHE (SERVES 10 TO 12)

INGREDIENTS

Caramel Crémeux

5 grams	½ tablespoon	unflavored gelatin powder
28 grams	2 tablespoons	water
923 grams	3¾ cups	whole milk
318 grams	1½ cups + 1 tablespoon	sugar
5 grams	1 teaspoon	vanilla extract
140 grams	7 large	egg yolks
63 grams	½ cup	cornstarch
5 grams	1½ teaspoons	salt
514 grams	4 sticks + 4 tablespoons (18 oz)	unsalted butter, cubed, at room temperature

Almond Nougatine

1.23 kilograms	13 cups	sliced almonds
1.54 kilograms	7¾ cups	sugar
77 grams	⅓ cup	water
1.23 kilograms	3⅓ cups	glucose
Cooking spray or vegetable oil		

Pâte à Choux

300 grams	1⅓ cups + ¼ cup	water
280 grams	1 cup + 4 teaspoons	whole milk
300 grams	2 sticks + 5 tablespoons (10½ oz)	unsalted butter, room temperature
12 grams	4 teaspoons	sugar
8 grams	4 teaspoons	salt
400 grams	2⅔ cups	all-purpose flour
600 to 700 grams	12 to 14 large	eggs

Egg Wash

| 50 grams | 1 large | egg |
| 20 grams | 1 large | egg yolk |

Caramel (for dipping)

1.33 kilograms	6⅓ cups	sugar
533 grams	2¼ cups	water
133 grams	⅓ cup + 1 tablespoon	glucose

Royal Icing (optional)

500 grams	4 cups	powdered sugar
10 grams	2 teaspoons	lemon juice
60 grams	2 large	egg whites

EQUIPMENT

Mixing bowls	Rubber or heatproof gloves
Medium pot	Rolling pin
Medium saucepan	8-inch (20 cm) nonstick round cake pan
Silicone spatula	Stand mixer
Whisk	Piping bags
Immersion blender (optional)	Plain round piping tip (at least ⅓ inch/1 cm in diameter)
Baking sheets	
Silicone baking mats or parchment paper	Pastry brush
Large pot	Large pot (at least 10- or 12-quart)
Digital thermometer	10-inch (25 cm) gold pastry board or 10-inch (25 cm) cake stand/round platter
Bench scraper or knife	

MAKE THE CARAMEL CRÉMEUX (DAY BEFORE)

1. Bloom the gelatin: In a small bowl, whisk together the gelatin and water until dissolved. Let the mixture sit a few minutes until the gelatin has bloomed (when it has absorbed the majority of the liquid, gaining 2 to 3 times its original volume, and feels firm and set).

recipe continues

2. Warm the milk: In a medium pot, bring the milk to a simmer over medium heat. Keep warm.

3. Make a dry caramel: Put the sugar in a small bowl and set it near the stove. Place a medium saucepan over medium heat. When the pan is hot, sprinkle a thin, even layer of sugar over the bottom of the pan. As the sugar melts and caramelizes, slowly sprinkle in more sugar, one small handful at a time, gently stirring with a silicone spatula and making sure each handful has reached an amber brown color before sprinkling in another handful. Once all the sugar has been added, cook until it has turned golden amber brown, 1 to 2 minutes. Remove from the heat immediately to keep it from burning.

* You can move the pan on and off the heat to control the temperature and make sure your sugar doesn't burn and instead stays a golden amber brown.

4. Temper the egg yolk mixture: In a bowl, whisk together the vanilla, egg yolks, and cornstarch. Gradually add one-third of the hot milk, whisking until combined.

5. Add hot milk to the caramel: Slowly pour the remaining hot milk into the pan of hot caramel (the caramel is still very hot and will bubble up once the milk is added, so pour it in little by little and be very careful!). Pour in the tempered yolk mixture and whisk until combined.

6. Cook the custard: Set the pan over medium heat and cook until it thickens, a few minutes. Remove from the heat.

7. Finish the crémeux and chill: In a large bowl, combine the gelatin mixture, salt, and cubed butter. Pour in the cooked custard, whisking until smooth and evenly combined and there are no lumps (you can also use an immersion blender). Cover with plastic wrap pressed against the surface to prevent a skin from forming and refrigerate until fully cool, a few hours or up to overnight.

MAKE THE ALMOND NOUGATINE (DAY BEFORE)*

* You will need a cool stone or marble countertop space to roll out the nougatine to at least 12 inches in diameter. This works best on a cool stone/ marble surface, as a metal or wood surface conducts too much heat.

8. Preheat the oven to 350°F (175°C). Line a baking sheet with a silicone baking mat or parchment paper. Line a second baking sheet with a silicone baking mat or parchment paper.

9. Warm the almonds: Spread the almonds on a lined baking sheet and warm in the oven for about 5 minutes, stirring them with a silicone spatula occasionally.* Once the almonds are warmed, leave the oven on so you can warm and soften the nougatine as needed as you're shaping it later on.

   While the almonds are warming, you'll make the caramel and you want the almonds to be warm when added to the caramel; if they are cold or room temperature, the temperature of the sugar syrup will drop too quickly.

10. Make the caramel: In a large pot, combine the sugar and water and bring to a boil over high heat, stirring occasionally with a silicone spatula. Once at a boil, reduce the heat to medium-high and add the glucose. Cook, stirring occasionally, until the mixture reaches 329°F (165°C) on a digital thermometer and becomes a light amber caramel color. You can move the pot on and off the heat as needed, swirling it to cook the caramel evenly. Remove from the heat.

11. Make the nougatine: Add the warm almonds to the hot caramel, folding with a silicone spatula until evenly coated.

12. Knead the nougatine: Spray a work surface with cooking spray (alternatively, grease the surface with a thin layer of vegetable oil). Turn the nougatine out onto the work surface. Using a bench scraper or knife, divide the nougatine in half. Work the one half with your hands, folding it over itself (you may need rubber/heatproof gloves as the nougatine will be very hot), until it's no longer runny and becomes firm but still pliable, like the texture of clay.

13. Make the croquembouche stand: Roll the nougatine into a large round that's about ⅓ inch (1 cm) thick. Using an 8-inch (20 cm) nonstick round cake pan as a guide, cut the nougatine into a round that's about 14 inches (35.5 cm) in diameter. Transfer the round into the cake pan, pushing it down into the bottom, into

recipe continues

the corners, and up the sides.* Trim off any excess along the top rim and let fully cool. This will become a stand for your croquembouche.

Work quickly, while the nougatine is still warm, soft, and pliable. Once the nougatine cools, it'll become hard and brittle. If you notice it's starting to harden and becomes tough to roll out/shape, place it on the second lined baking sheet and return it to the oven, along with the excess trimmings, to resoften as needed.

14. **Make the croquembouche base:** Roll out more nougatine (rewarming it in the oven on the lined baking sheet as needed, and reworking it on the greased countertop until firm but pliable) to a large round about ⅓ inch (1 cm) thick. Again using the cake pan as a guide, cut the nougatine into a round that's about 9½ inches (24 cm) in diameter. This will serve as the base for your croquembouche.

15. **Make the nougatine decorations:** Roll out more nougatine (rewarming and reworking it as needed) into a long rectangle about 20 × 4 inches (50 × 10 cm) and ⅓ inch (1 cm) thick. Make alternating diagonal cuts to create individual triangles. These will be used to decorate around the croquembouche.

16. Carefully unmold the nougatine stand in the cake pan (at this point, it should have fully cooled and hardened). Set aside all the nougatine pieces in a cool and dry place, covered in plastic wrap, until ready to assemble the croquembouche.

MAKE THE PÂTE À CHOUX

17. Position two racks in the the oven and preheat the oven to 285°F (140°C). Line two baking sheets with silicone baking mats or parchment paper.

18. **Make the dough:** In a large pot, combine the water, milk, butter, sugar, and salt and bring to a boil over medium heat, stirring occasionally. Add the flour and stir vigorously with a spatula until a dough comes together, a few minutes. Cook, stirring, until a thin film starts to form at the bottom of the saucepan as the result of the dough sticking, 1 to 2 minutes. Keep going until a white film completely covers the bottom of the pan, which should take about 5 more minutes. Remove from the heat.

19. Add the eggs: Transfer the dough to a stand mixer fitted with the paddle. With the mixer on medium speed, paddle the dough to let off some heat and steam for 4 to 5 minutes. Then begin to add the eggs one at a time, mixing until each egg is fully incorporated before adding the next one. You'll add 600 to 700 grams of eggs (12 to 14 large eggs).* The outside of the bowl should be hot to the touch, but bearable.

When making pâte à choux, the number of eggs needed will vary. The consistency of the dough dictates how many eggs should be added. Sometimes the dough dries out a bit more in the pan and can take on more eggs. To check, stick a spatula into the dough and lift it high above the bowl. The dough should fall slowly off the spatula in ribbons. It should feel thick, but fluid enough to pipe.

20. Pipe the dough: Using a spatula, place two large scoops of the warm choux dough into a piping bag fitted with a large plain tip (at least ⅓ inch/1 cm in diameter), filling it one-third full. Push the dough down toward the tip of the bag. Holding the piping bag at a 90-degree angle about ½ inch (1.3 cm) above the prepared baking sheet, pipe rounds of choux dough about 1½ inches (4 cm) in diameter, spacing them about 1 inch (2.5 cm) apart. Gently smooth/flatten the pointed tips of the rounds with your fingers.

21. Brush with egg wash: In a small bowl, beat together the egg and egg yolk. Using a pastry brush (or the tips of your fingers), lightly brush the egg wash over the choux.

22. Bake the choux: Bake the choux until golden brown, light to the touch, and hollow when broken open, 30 to 35 minutes, rotating the pan front to back halfway through the baking time. Let the choux fully cool.

23. Once the choux are fully cooled, gently lift and remove them from the parchment.

recipe continues

24. Fill the choux with caramel crémeux: Remove the chilled caramel crémeux from the fridge. Using a rubber spatula, place two big scoops of crémeux into a piping bag. Snip off the very tip of piping bag so the opening is about ¼ inch (6 mm) in diameter. Use the tip of the piping bag (or a small paring knife) to pierce a hole into the bottom of each choux, pressing on the bag to fill each choux with crémeux. Continue until you've filled all the choux.*

* You'll need at least 53 crémeux-filled choux to build the croquembouche. This recipe will give you extra choux and cream; you can always fill a dozen or so more to have backups, and place the extras in the center of the croquembouche as you're building it to help stabilize the tower.

MAKE THE CARAMEL (FOR DIPPING)

25. In a medium pot, combine the water and sugar and bring to a boil over high heat, stirring occasionally.

26. Once at a boil, reduce the heat to medium-high and add the glucose. Cook until the mixture reaches 329°F (165°C), as measured with a digital thermometer, and becomes a light amber color. You can move the pot on and off the heat as needed, swirling it to cook the caramel evenly. Remove from the heat and start building the croquembouche.

27. Assemble the croquembouche: Line a baking sheet with a silicone baking mat or parchment paper.

28. Place the nougatine base on a 10-inch (25 cm) gold pastry board or a 10-inch (25 cm) cake stand/round platter (you can use a bit of glucose or caramel to stick the nougatine onto the base to keep it in place).

29. Center the round nougatine stand over the nougatine base, with the flat surface on top.*

* If the edges of the stand are jagged/uneven, you can use a Microplane or small grater to smooth them out.

recipe continues

30. Dip the choux in caramel: Carefully dip the top of each choux, one at a time, into the hot caramel. Set each dipped choux on the baking sheet, caramel side up.* (Be careful: The caramel is very hot. You may want to wear rubber/heatproof gloves to protect your hands.) Repeat until you've dipped all the choux. Allow them to fully cool and set (the caramel on top of each choux should harden), a few minutes.

  * *If the caramel in the pot begins to harden as you are dipping the choux, rewarm it over very low heat, stirring with a silicone spatula occasionally, until it becomes a liquid again.*

31. Build the tower: Dip the side of one of the choux into the caramel and place it just inside the edge of the nougatine stand, with the hardened caramel side facing out (the hot caramel will serve as the "glue" to attach the choux to the base and to each other). Repeat with more choux, dipping the sides with caramel and arranging them in a circle that follows the shape of the nougatine stand. This first base layer should fit about 10 choux. Repeat to form a second tier, this time with 9 choux. Continue with more tiers, with 1 fewer choux per tier as you make your way up, until you've formed a tower with a single choux on top.*

  * *Sometimes you can do 3 choux on top and then add a flower decoration of your choice.*

32. Decorate the base: Place the nougatine triangles around the base layer of choux, dipping the ends into the caramel in order to "glue" them into place.

MAKE THE ROYAL ICING (IF USING)

33. In a stand mixer fitted with the whisk (or a hand mixer), combine the powdered sugar, lemon juice, and egg whites and mix until light and fluffy. If the mixture feels a bit dry, add a few drops of water as needed to make a smooth consistency. Cover the bowl with plastic wrap if you're not immediately using it so the icing doesn't dry out.

34. Pipe decorations: Transfer the royal icing to a piping bag. Snip off the tip of the piping bag to form a small hole. Pipe the icing around the seam of the nougatine stand (where it meets the base) and on the edges of the triangle pieces in a decorative pattern.

35. To serve: Allow the caramel to fully set and harden and the royal icing to fully harden. Serve the croquembouche and enjoy!

STORAGE

Best enjoyed immediately.

Acknowledgments

Jessica Cheng: For organizing, pushing, reminding me of deadlines, and tracking me down (our second book together!).

Evan Sung: For always seeing the light and beauty in our creations.

Maeve Sheridan: For knowing there are a million different plates and spoons, but only a few that are perfect.

Mary Dodd: For testing our recipes at home and asking the questions that made them better.

Kiki, Luca, Nico, Liv, and Pisi: My favorite dessert-loving kids, who filled this book with your smiles and laughter. Someday you all will change the world.

Index

NOTE: Page references in *italics* indicate photographs.

About the Author

In 2011, James Beard Award–winning pastry chef **Dominique Ansel** opened his first shop, the eponymous Dominique Ansel Bakery in New York City's SoHo neighborhood, with just four employees, and he has since shaken up the pastry world with the innovation and creativity at the heart of his work. He's been responsible for creating some of the most celebrated pastries in the world, including the Cronut® (named one of *Time* magazine's "25 Best Inventions of the Year 2013"), Cookie Shot, Frozen S'mores, Blossoming Hot Chocolate, and more. For his prolific creativity, he was named the World's Best Pastry Chef in 2017 by the World's 50 Best Restaurants awards. *Food & Wine* has called him a "confectionary Van Gogh," while the *New York Post* named him the "Willy Wonka of NYC." The prestigious Ordre du Mérite Agricole, France's second highest honor, has also been bestowed upon him. He is the author of two other cookbooks: *Dominique Ansel: The Secret Recipes* and *Everyone Can Bake: Simple Recipes to Master and Mix*.